Carolyn Fa

"The markets taught us lessons I hope we never forget. McKnight weaves those lessons into a book that allows us to see into the future of our new business ideas. The next big thing needs to stand on solid financial ground, and that's where McKnight steps in to help tomorrow's innovators and entrepreneurs."

—U.S. Rep. Michael G. Oxley (Fourth Ohio District)
Co-author, Sarbanes-Oxley Act of 2002

"This book could only have been crafted in the crucible of launching new businesses in the classroom, something about which I have considerable experience. Clearly, McKnight has touched upon 44 critical elements of success and if you can score well, you could be on your way to a huge win. Buy it, use it, and keep it on your desk for repeated reference. It is indeed that good."

—Dr. John W. Altman
Robert E. Weissman Professor, Babson College and
Vice President, Ewing Marion Kauffman Foundation

"McKnight's work involves creating new businesses in the classroom and it is not a surprise to see a tool as effective as 'Innovators Scorecard' grow from his teaching. The class could not proceed without a hard hitting up front screen for all the ideas the students would bring into the room."

—Professor Murray B. Low
Lang Center for Entrepreneurship, Columbia Business School

"This Scorecard is a great analytical tool. Had it been available a few years ago, we could have saved ourselves about $5 billion."

—Robert J. Wussler
President and CEO, Ted Turner Pictures

"Over the boom and bust of the late 1990s and first couple of years of the 21st century, it is clear that a tool such as McKnight's 'Innovator's Scorecard' would have saved the country many billions of dollars in losses and heartache. Every venture capitalist, lawyer, and accountant should require their new venture clients to score well before they commit their valuable resources."

—Thomas Curley
former President, *USA Today*

In an increasingly competitive world, it is quality
of thinking that gives an edge—an idea that opens new
doors, a technique that solves a problem, or an insight
that simply helps make sense of it all.

We work with leading authors in the various arenas
of business and finance to bring cutting-edge thinking
and best learning practice to a global market.

It is our goal to create world-class print publications
and electronic products that give readers
knowledge and understanding which can then be
applied, whether studying or at work.

To find out more about our business
products, you can visit us at www.ft-ph.com

Will It Fly?

How to Know if Your New Business Idea Has Wings ... Before You Take the Leap

Thomas K. McKnight

FINANCIAL TIMES
Prentice Hall

An Imprint of Pearson Education
London ▪ New York ▪ San Francisco ▪ Toronto ▪ Sydney
Tokyo ▪ Singapore ▪ Hong Kong ▪ Cape Town ▪ Madrid
Paris ▪ Milan ▪ Munich ▪ Amsterdam

Editorial/production supervision: *Kathleen M. Caren*
Art director: *Gail Cocker-Bogusz*
Cover design director: *Jerry Votta*
Cover design: *Nina Scuderi*
Manufacturing manager: *Alexis R. Heydt-Long*
Marketing manager: *Laura Bulcher*
Executive editor: *James Boyd*
Editorial assistant: *Linda Ramagnano*

© 2004 Prentice Hall PTR
Pearson Education, Inc.
Upper Saddle River, New Jersey 07458

Printed in the United States of America
10 9 8 7 6 5 4 3 2 1

ISBN 0-13--046221-7

Pearson Education LTD.
Pearson Education Australia PTY, Limited
Pearson Education Singapore, Pte. Ltd.
Pearson Education North Asia Ltd.
Pearson Education Canada, Ltd.
Pearson Educación de Mexico, S.A. de C.V.
Pearson Education—Japan
Pearson Education Malaysia, Pte. Ltd.

This book is dedicated to the most wonderful soul I ever knew,
a fellow who taught high school in Milford, Ohio, and Mason, Ohio
for 30 years, and who was a U.S. Marine in the middle of the
Pacific Ocean on December 7, 1941. His name was
Charles R. McKnight and he was my Dad.
I miss him so.

FINANCIAL TIMES PRENTICE HALL BOOKS

For more information, please go to www.ft-ph.com

Business and Technology

Sarv Devaraj and Rajiv Kohli
> *The IT Payoff: Measuring the Business Value of Information Technology Investments*

Nicholas D. Evans
> *Business Innovation and Disruptive Technology: Harnessing the Power of Breakthrough Technology…for Competitive Advantage*

Nicholas D. Evans
> *Consumer Gadgets: 50 Ways to Have Fun and Simplify Your Life with Today's Technology…and Tomorrow's*

Faisal Hoque
> *The Alignment Effect: How to Get Real Business Value Out of Technology*

Economics

David Dranove
> *What's Your Life Worth? Health Care Rationing…Who Lives? Who Dies? Who Decides?*

John C. Edmunds
> *Brave New Wealthy World: Winning the Struggle for World Prosperity*

Jonathan Wight
> *Saving Adam Smith: A Tale of Wealth, Transformation, and Virtue*

Entrepreneurship

Oren Fuerst and Uri Geiger
> *From Concept to Wall Street: A Complete Guide to Entrepreneurship and Venture Capital*

David Gladstone and Laura Gladstone
> *Venture Capital Handbook: An Entrepreneur's Guide to Raising Venture Capital, Revised and Updated*

Thomas K. McKnight
> *Will It Fly? How to Know if Your New Business Idea Has Wings… Before You Take the Leap*

Erica Orloff and Kathy Levinson, Ph.D.
> *The 60-Second Commute: A Guide to Your 24/7 Home Office Life*

Jeff Saperstein and Daniel Rouach
> *Creating Regional Wealth in the Innovation Economy: Models, Perspectives, and Best Practices*

Stephen Spinelli, Jr., Robert M. Rosenberg, and Sue Birley
> *Franchising: Pathway to Wealth Creation*

Leadership

Jim Despain and Jane Bodman Converse
  And Dignity for All: Unlocking Greatness through Values-Based Leadership
Marshall Goldsmith, Vijay Govindarajan, Beverly Kaye, and Albert A. Vicere
  The Many Facets of Leadership
Marshall Goldsmith, Cathy Greenberg, Alastair Robertson, and Maya Hu-Chan
  Global Leadership: The Next Generation

Management

Rob Austin and Lee Devin
  Artful Making: What Managers Need to Know About How Artists Work
J. Stewart Black and Hal B. Gregersen
  Leading Strategic Change: Breaking Through the Brain Barrier
William C. Byham, Audrey B. Smith, and Matthew J. Paese
  Grow Your Own Leaders: How to Identify, Develop, and Retain Leadership Talent
David M. Carter and Darren Rovell
  On the Ball: What You Can Learn About Business from Sports Leaders
Subir Chowdhury
  Organization 21C: Someday All Organizations Will Lead this Way
Ross Dawson
  *Living Networks: Leading Your Company, Customers, and Partners
  in the Hyper-connected Economy*
Charles J. Fombrun and Cees B.M. Van Riel
  Fame and Fortune: How Successful Companies Build Winning Reputations
Amir Hartman
  Ruthless Execution: What Business Leaders Do When Their Companies Hit the Wall
Harvey A. Hornstein
  *The Haves and the Have Nots: The Abuse of Power and Privilege in the Workplace…
  and How to Control It*
Kevin Kennedy and Mary Moore
  Going the Distance: Why Some Companies Dominate and Others Fail
Robin Miller
  The Online Rules of Successful Companies: The Fool-Proof Guide to Building Profits
Fergus O'Connell
  The Competitive Advantage of Common Sense: Using the Power You Already Have
W. Alan Randolph and Barry Z. Posner
  *Checkered Flag Projects: 10 Rules for Creating and Managing Projects that Win,
  Second Edition*
Stephen P. Robbins
  Decide & Conquer: Make Winning Decisions to Take Control of Your Life
Stephen P. Robbins
  The Truth About Managing People…And Nothing but the Truth

Contents

PREFACE

All Great Ideas Are Worth Their Weight in Gold

This book introduces the *Innovator's Scorecard*. It is a highly intuitive tool that allows a quick, snapshot evaluation of a business idea. It is calculated to measure the worthiness of an idea before critical resources are tapped or engaged. By scoring your idea with this index, you will identify its strengths and weaknesses. You will know whether your business will fly, how to make it fly higher, and how to add the weight necessary to drive it successfully into the market so you win your share of the gold.

Over the past seven years, Columbia University, Georgetown University, the University of Maryland, the University of Denver, the University of North Dakota, and The George Washington University have periodically offered a course in entrepreneurship that requires students to bring their business ideas to class. The essence of the course was also taught 16 times in Russia to senior executives of various petroleum companies, all by means of a real-time language translator and all under the aegis of Columbia University. This book describes the distilled synthesis of a key element of those courses: a comprehensive, common-sense tool that can quickly assess the viability and feasibility of an idea at the very earliest moments of each course. In each course, the students tried to launch their ideas into real live companies. That tool, which became known first as the "Launch Aperture" and later as the "Innovator's Scorecard," is the basis of this book. We needed an up-front device that would instantly align and screen the ideas for the students to manipulate during the course. Did it work? Absolutely. Students were bringing in checks for tens of thousands of dollars from customers long before the business plans were written. In one case, the students closed on $456 million for the support of their classroom project.

Anyone who uses the Innovator's Scorecard—from a first-time-at-bat owner to a repeat entrepreneur to a lawyer to a seasoned investor—can tell immediately whether an idea has the silhouette of a success story. Using a prelaunch assessment tool is of vital importance—each year, there are heavy economic losses attributable to the failure of businesses. For example, Dr. Stephen C. Perry's study of the relationship between business planning (or lack thereof) and the failure of businesses in the United States turned up this factoid: Each year, 17,000 businesses fail, and the aggregate losses accrue to $40 billion.[1] This is a staggering sum. By acting as

---

1. Stephen C. Perry, "The Relationship between Written Business Plans and the Failure of Small Businesses in the U.S." *Journal of Small Business Management* 39(3), p. 205, 2001.

a silent advisor at the very beginning of the thought process, the Innovator's Scorecard helps would-be entrepreneurs reason through the facts that are known or that can be surmised up front. The entrepreneur can then predict the success or failure of his or her venture long before any serious money, savings, or resources are committed or spent. *Will it Fly?* is likely to be the best investment any entrepreneur ever made.

Acknowledgements

If this book helps anyone, Prentice Hall and I owe you a special thanks for buying the book and you owe a special thanks to some people who made it possible.

Here are just a few of the luminaries: a *magna cum laude* thanks goes to Columbia University and its many wonderful souls, including my friends, Dr. Carl Pavarini for his insightful teaching and recommendations to organize the book as you now see it; Joe Rubin for the organization and support of all those amazing classes in the oil fields of Siberia and Izhevsk; Doctors Eli Noam and Murray Low for their guidance and support; Meyer Feldberg for his remarkable leadership of the Graduate Business School and who made it such a dream to work with the masters; Dace Udris, who could fix any problem with her magical "dose of Dace"; and frankly, the entire faculty, administration, and students of a unique academic institution that seemed to absolutely resonate around amiable and brilliant cooperation from top to bottom.

Not to be forgotten are Ian MacMillan of Wharton fame (he is the Chair of the University of Pennsylvania's entrepreneurship program who alerted me that Prentice Hall could be interested in *Will It Fly?*) and Elaine Romanelli of Georgetown University fame (she is the Chair of their entrepreneurship program), both of whom have their own connect points with Columbia.

Writing books takes lots of quiet time and a special thanks goes to the University of North Dakota for suffering with a one-term lecturer while I snuck off between classes to write this book. A special thanks goes to Dr. John Vitton, chair of UND's management department, who is in his mid-seventies, still plays in an ice hockey league every Thursday night (he founded the ice hockey program at Ohio State and he's as tough as a railroad spike), and who would *not* let me teach anywhere else. My graduate assistant, Becky Haakenson, a.k.a. "Radar," gets a rousing special thanks for making it a joy to teach by tackling the administrative burden and for helping with my "value grading."

Bruce Downey, CEO of Barr Laboratories, wins a special thanks for his steadfast friendship and encouragement from our days long ago in that pretty fraternity house at Miami University.

A special thanks goes to son Jonathan for his constant elbowing to teach and write the book (he will someday write his own book on dogged persistence); daughter Katie for her wickedly funny and supportive ebullience (viz. "Hey Dad, why don't they print and sell conception cards along with birthday cards?"); Marian, my pal and wife who gave me a safe harbor while I wrote the book; and of course, Mom (Ann McKnight who is holding forth in Cincinnati) who is basking in the renown from her 1949 photographic masterpiece shown on the cover of this book, and who taught me to love twiddling with words.

Finally, the most important special thanks could go to the intrepid students who took the courses! You were all absolute treasures and I hope you all harvest your own idea some day soon.

Carpe diem

—Tom McKnight

August 2003

Part I

OVERVIEW

Before we begin, there are many ways to go into business for yourself. Consulting; acquiring a professional license to practice law, medicine, or accounting; buying a franchise; or taking over the family business all work. This book is for people who wish to pursue a new idea or innovation that responds to a need customers are waiting to have solved. It is also about finding an idea that has a high likelihood of someday being worth a considerable amount of money.

Another consideration before we get started is the personal circumstances of the entrepreneur. If you are starting a new business, it takes time. This goes for all new businesses, frankly, so it should come as no surprise. Securities and mortgage brokerage, law, medicine, and accounting are all demanding exercises in the first lean years. Starting a new company is the same idea. You must build support for your product and then enjoy the fruit of your work. If you are raising money for your business, remember that the investor is not likely to allow you to walk away with a substantial salary until you have proven yourself and your products. The point is that if you are unemployed and considering a new venture as a possible means by which to support the family, be realistic. It could take longer than you think for you to bring home enough dollars to cover all the bills. The key is to calculate carefully the distance between today and that moment when you will receive cash remuneration. If it takes one month to land a great job for every $10,000 in salary you are seeking, you have a rough rule of thumb against which to measure your chances. For those of you who believe that you are a victim of discrimination, the odds shift even more dramatically against your being hired soon.

Allow me to introduce my co-teacher. I have always used this wise owl to help teach my classes because he or she (I could never figure out the gender of my co-teacher) is absolutely, positively never wrong. Our co-teacher inspires great respect from me and the students. Ladies and gentlemen, meet Dr. Market:

 From time to time Dr. Market will offer special insight into a particular matter, garnered after years of experience in the field of new venture launching. Here is its very first observation: It is difficult to conjure up any business idea that cannot be grown to a logical and large critical mass. Let's look at golf caddying and seamstress work. Can they be grown to a greater scale and provide you with greater net worth and income? Absolutely. The golf caddying can grow into an institute with training, certification, distinctive jumpers or uniforms, and PGA/LPGA endorsement. The seamstress business can grow with training, licensing, practice standards, and possibly a trade association for independents that will register their voices in the congress and state legislatures. This book addresses the potential for bigger and better businesses at the very moment an idea pops into your mind. It does not address the possibility of keeping your business a solitary, one-person-band.

Finding the Right Idea

Let's pause for a moment and examine how people find ideas to pursue. The process of finding the right idea involves several questions that you should ask yourself and your friends. They can be answered from experience or personal knowledge. The first question is so important that it is one of the 44 elements of the Scorecard, and you will see it again soon. The other questions are calculated to trigger a thought in your mind, maybe several. The objective of this chapter is to help you find one or several ideas that are worthy of analysis with the Innovator's Scorecard.

Dr. Market's Observation:

 Don't just quit with one idea! The Innovator's Scorecard is so quick and efficient that you should be able to analyze a number of ideas simultaneously. In my classes we routinely analyzed between 10 and 20 ideas and the students selected the ones that scored the highest, all in the limited confines of one class session.

---

1. Identify a Compelling Unserved Need

Here is the most potent of the idea-generating tactics. It can be a two-step process: the first step is to create a list of people you know who have a great understanding about some field of endeavor. Find as many people as you can who know much about a subject or industry you might be interested in pursuing, even if it is in the nonprofit sector. What friends of yours have worked for a significant period of time in their field? Easy question—you should know people who fill this description. Now that you have the list, here is the question to ask the people on it: "What compelling unserved (or underserved) need do you perceive in your specialty?"

Let them think it over—often it can take a few days. Don't be embarrassed to inquire about others who might be able to help, particularly if your contact has no answer for you.

It does not matter whether you are a suddenly unemployed janitor, secretary, senior executive, insurance adjuster, lawyer, or politician. Everyone knows people who know a lot about something. In other words, there are no excuses for not being able to turn up a great idea using this process. If you do this for one week and you approach one or two dozen people who really know what they are doing in some field, you will have at least one and most likely several ideas that could make you rich.

Dr. Market's Observation:

 When you ask whether an industry has a compelling unserved or underserved need, you don't have to understand a thing about the business. That understanding will come in time. The key for now is finding an area in which you would feel comfortable working. Frankly, the older you are the more likely you will tap an old experience that could illuminate the trail of highest promise. I know a person who performed title examinations between college and law school, worked briefly as a real estate broker and then as a stock broker, and finally ended up creating a blockbuster financial services firm that brokered mortgages and registered securities all in the same transactions. In the middle 20 years he was doing something completely unrelated.

---

2. Identify an Irritation

Another tactic is to accumulate a list of the things that really annoy you or your friends. Poor service at the cable company, egg cartons that hold a dozen eggs instead of four, five-day bank holds on out-of-town checks, a confrontation with someone at the airline ticket counter, pop-up advertisements in your Web browser, impossible congestion at the screening areas of the local airport, the high price of air travel to certain cities, and so forth. List all of these irritations. It is not yet time to discard any idea. Believe it or not, there are remarkable new business venture potentials in each of these possibilities. I suggest you try this for one week, taking notes. You should come away with some serious candidates for further examination.

3. Look for "Sleeves Off the Vests" Potential
The old saw about "sleeves off the vests" can reveal some suggestions for a new business.[1] Do you know of any business that has refuse or byproducts that are already manufactured or built and that are being discarded? Nothing is too insignificant for consideration. Natural gas being burned off the oil fields in Siberia was the inspiration to build a compact yet powerful electricity generation plant powered by that same natural gas. The same logic might apply to the events, people, and equipment that accumulate around a great ski lodge. What could you do with them in the summer? The key here is being alert to downtime or materials that go to waste. Do any ideas spring to mind?

4. React to Jealousy
Jealousy can be yet another inspiration for a new business idea. Can you see some product or service that you can or should be offering except that someone else has "beaten you to the punch?"

---

1. Somewhere way back in the lore of business is the wisdom of selling the sleeves from the manufacture of vests. It refers to the fact that the clothing manufacturer was able to use the cloth saved from not being used for sleeves and applying it to some other product. Never mind that the savings would pass directly to the vest manufacturing activities. It was the *image* of sleeves laying around the cutting room floor that was the source of the wisdom.

When Orion Satellite Corporation applied to the FCC for permission to compete with Intelsat (the international telecommunications satellite cartel),[2] it didn't take long for the late, great, Rene Anselmo to seek "me-too" authority to do the same thing with his PanAmSat. At least he had the decency to buy us lunch at The Palm before he filed. Be careful here, however, because you will derive some low scores in many critical elements of the Scorecard. Don't be surprised if your idea that is born out of jealousy fails to achieve a passing score. Try to restrict your jealousies to persons or enterprises and not products. Do any ideas spring to mind?

5. Find a New Technology or a New Use for an Existing Technology

Within the past 20 years, we have witnessed the advent of PCs, Macs, cellular phones, direct broadcast satellites, 500 channels of video on cable and satellite, the Internet, email, three-pound laptops, and much, much more. What is coming next? My guess is that the next 20 years will see things we can hardly imagine now. Is there a new technology out there that can be tapped? Is there an ancillary development or application to any new technology that offers the potential for a new industry or business? Examples could include developing new sensor hardware and software for PCs, creating video stringing software for cell phones, or establishing an Internet service provider (ISP) in a foreign country and selling computers with your software (and access number) imbedded in each. Can you see a new technology blooming overseas? Do any ideas spring to mind?

6. Imagine a Scene You'd Like to See

Think about *Mad Magazine*, a cultural icon in which a cartoonist would draw a picture of a commonly understood situation or

---

2. For further explanation see Appendix I.

dilemma alongside a perfectly preposterous solution. Expand on that mischievous notion: can you envision a circumstance or situation in industry or everyday life that allows you to conjure up a "scene you'd like to see?" This line of reasoning is allowed to be wacky because the underlying objective is to find a path to riches that no one else has pursued. Can you spin the earth differently? Can you flatten a mountain? Can you make commercial use of a signal bounced off the moon? Can you launch a discount airline? The objective is to uncover an idea worthy of pursuit and sometimes it requires moving off in an odd direction. Never believe that "preposterousness" thwarts new ventures.[3] Quite the contrary, it can have a role in ensuring success. Do any ideas spring to mind?

7. Get People to Say "Holy Smoke!"

What could be done with a new product or service that would cause people to stand back and mutter "holy smoke?" We will worry later about reason and practicality; for now we just want to uncover an extraordinary product or service. Is there a surprise somewhere? Remember that this exercise is calculated to trigger new ideas for consideration. Here are some "holy smokes":

- Undertaking supersonic travel with no sonic boom

- Moving a smell across the Internet

- Creating a device on which to see full sight, sound, motion, color, high definition, 3-D video

- Communicating by thought

---

3. This undercurrent of mischief in entrepreneurship has roots in the teachings of the one fellow who is widely viewed as the father of learning about entrepreneurship, Dr. Joseph Schumpeter. His views on the subject of "creative destruction" can be seen in Appendix III.

The Innovator's Scorecard has an uncanny feature: If you lob an idea into the analysis in a field in which you hope to succeed, you will probably find that a slightly different and much more potent idea emerges. The Scorecard will actually refine or groom your idea into one that has the maximum potential for success. If there is any hope at all for your idea to win, the path to success should become evident in the analysis. The point is this: You don't need to come up with the winning idea to launch your analysis. Try a "Hail Mary" lob and you are likely to walk away with a winner that is different from what you expected.

Dr. Market's Observation:

 Remember the happy factor. By now you should have at least a couple of ideas to pursue, maybe several. Pause for a moment and clear out the ones you simply cannot imagine yourself ever doing. For example, I always thought that the ownership and management of a portable toilet business would be a lucrative deal with solid margins and plenty of work. But I just couldn't imagine myself doing it...You get the point. If there are good ideas on your list better left to someone else to pursue, so be it. Make sure your happy factor will not be abused.

Finally, it's time to score your ideas. Prepare a one-paragraph description of each idea, and then run each of them through the Innovator's Scorecard as explained in the next chapter and in the 44 elements that follow. It should take about 15 to 30 minutes per idea and at the end of each analysis you will have a score. With added time and thought, the scores are likely to improve somewhat in accuracy, particularly after you wrestle with them over the course of several days.

The Scorecard Elements

Compelling Unserved Need	Delivery Advantages
Explainable Uniqueness	Resources Available
Sustainable Differentiation	Preemption & Domination
Demonstrable Now	Strategy to Penetrate Market
Good Competition	Strategy for Breaching the Chasm
Bad Competition	Proprietary Ownership
Compelling Pricing Possible	Partnering Candidates
Closable Customers	Appropriateness of Location
Quality of Evidence of Demand	Quality of Backup Plan
Ahead of the Market	Unfair Advantages
Ambush Exposure	Manageable Capital Requirements
"Hot Market"	Low Capital Required
Attitude of Confidence	Until Launch
and Fearlessness	Visible Capital
Commitment	High Potential Value
Staying Power	Foreseeable Harvest
Passion	Taboo
Management Competence	Lack of Showstoppers
Honesty and Integrity	Pretending Not to Know
Success Ethic	High-Profile Persons Available
Looking Good in the Lobby	Punchy, Compelling Story
Cash Flowing Now	Government Relevance
Revenue Model That Swamps Costs	Low-Hanging Fruit

Each of the 44 elements in the Innovator's Scorecard will measure a specific aspect of your idea. The Scorecard, which is also downloadable at http://www.prenhall.com/willitfly/, can be seen in Appendix IV—you can calculate with it by hand with a simple calculator or you can enter the values and formulae into an Excel spreadsheet.[4] The scoring of each element varies according to

---

4. Don't forget to test your spreadsheet by entering 10s for each score—the total should equal 860. Divide that number into your idea's weighted aggregate score to determine your grade. A 70 or more is passing.

the subject matter of the idea. In the next few paragraphs we will explore the role of intuition, how to score and weigh the elements, a bonus method of using the Scorecard, how to deal with a bad score in an element, adjusting your scoring if an item is truly irrelevant, maintaining reality, synthesizing the scores, and dealing with overlap, that is, the possibility that two or more elements seem to be covering the same concept. Once we grasp these administrative details, we explore the various sections that are presented in each element. Each element has an actual scoring sample at the end so that you will understand how it can be applied to a real-life situation. Occasionally I will need to make assumptions that would be based upon my personal experience, such as my political contacts or my access to capital. I will describe these assumptions and disguise the names.

Subjectivity and the Role of Intuition

In the first few precious moments of an idea's existence, a struggle emerges between objectivity and subjectivity. If you were perfectly objective, you might just toss away a very good idea. Perhaps objectivity can be thought of as an offshoot of the strategic planning process.

The key to the Innovator's Scorecard is therefore *intuition*, which *Webster's Dictionary* defines as "the act by which the mind perceives the truth of things immediately without reasoning and deduction, a truth that cannot be acquired by, but is assumed in experience." In a world that honors research and objective analysis, the possibility that a purely intuitive tool could be helpful is intriguing.

Clearly, the objectivity[5] that results from due diligence investigations has a place in the decision-making process. However, it is fair to say that nearly every important innovation took its first steps on the

---

5. Unfortunately the objective (that is, non-intuitive) approach to new enterprises as practiced in corporate America is sometimes vulnerable to corporate politics. For whatever reason, when large corporations try to launch new businesses, rational judgment sometimes is trumped by politics in the executive suite. Motorola's experience with Iridium is exhibit A. To professionals outside the company, Iridium simply never made sense as a commercial venture.

basis of subjectivity and intuition. General Motors, AT&T, Motorola, Procter & Gamble and nearly every other Fortune 500 name began with little more than a hunch. Before the first automobile, phone call, portable radio transceiver, or bar of soap was ever sold, the prospect of success was 100% in the minds of the developers.

There are some remarkable success stories involving lesser-known endeavors, too. One of the most curious involves the US Navy submarine USS Scorpion (SSN-589), which sank May 22, 1968, and was discovered about six months later in more than 10,000 feet of water about 400 miles southwest of the Azores. The submarine was found after several highly experienced naval design experts and mathematicians guessed at the location in a betting exercise conducted by John Craven, the civilian specialist that the Navy hired to manage the investigation. The consensus opinion was that a torpedo motor had been activated, and that to activate its internal switch to turn the engine off, the submarine had reversed course precisely 180 degrees. Based upon their collective hunch, the submarine was found about 200 yards from the designated coordinates.[6] Intuition solved the puzzle.

The Numbers on the Scorecard

Here is the description of the two numbering schemes used for each element. The first is scoring and the second is the weighting. Scores are unique to each business idea, while the weights are identical for each element for all business ideas.

Scoring

The scoring continuum runs from +10 to –10. The first challenge is to determine whether the score is positive or negative. Essentially, this means evaluating the risks and rewards of a certain action or

---

6. Sherry Sontag et al, *Blind Mans Bluff: The Untold Story of American Submarine Espionage*, Chapter 5, Thorndike Press, 2000.

behavior. You may not realize it, but that is something you do every day: What are the odds that I will maneuver around a slow poke if I were to take the far-right lane on the freeway? Would I be happier if I were to use the other cleaners? Should I overstay my welcome on a parking meter? In each of these cases we assess the odds of success against the penalty for failure.

Importantly, you must comfort yourself that a feeling you have about a particular score is sufficient. This is a critical component of the intuitive: the educated guess. You can always adjust the score later if after further consideration your score would "feel better" if it were adjusted. How do I score each element? I begin with a pass/fail mark, a 7 being the magic threshold. Does it deserve a score above 7? How much? Is it C (7), B (8), or A (9) level work? Is it a perfect 10? Since nearly all readers have had experience with this scale, it should be a manageable scoring proposition. If it is a flunk, is it a close 6? Or does it plunge down through a 5 (that is, a 50%), 4, or a 3? Does it deserve a flat zero, as in no possible way? Does it deserve something slightly more than a zero, say a 1 or a 2? I give a 1 or a 2 to elements that deserve a zero but that also have some redeeming value.

Some scores can be so low—even for ventures that ultimately are successful—that even zero is inadequate and we score the idea in the negative range. For example, Orion Satellite Corporation proposed to compete in international satellite telecommunications with a global cartel named Intelsat. The US representative and connecting service, Comsat, which owned the exclusive authority to operate into and from Intelsat satellites, was charging roughly 10 times the price of domestic satellite services for basically identical technology. At Orion we were convinced that we could provide a better service for a fraction of the price. But still, with 130 nations aligned against it, Orion deserved a dramatically bad score on the element called Showstoppers. In other words, if an element is not merely weak but rather a colossal handicap, it deserves a score in negative territory. If this element deserves a score indicating absolute certain death, score it a −10. We'll return to Orion's Showstopper score later.

Weighting

Each element has a unique "weight" that deserves to be multiplied against the score. This "weighting" is an acknowledgment that some elements are of heavier "weight" or importance than others. Rather than delve into a long explanation of precise weighting, I have taken the liberty of simply assigning a light, medium, or heavy weighting to each element. Naturally, if an element has no weight or relevance at all, it will not be found on the Scorecard. If the weight is light, medium, or heavy, the score will be multiplied by 1, 2, or 3. In keeping with the intuitive nature of the Scorecard, this weighting is simply a feeling based upon my experience. The individual weights of each element remain constant for all ideas, while the scoring of each element will naturally be quite different for each idea. For example, every time you score a Critical Unserved Need, that score will be weighted a 3 irrespective of whether you are launching a new airline or a nursing home.

A Bonus

In addition to rating the viability of a new venture, the Innovator's Scorecard can be used years later as a diagnostic tune-up tool.[7] As experience mounts and the entrepreneur accumulates and synthesizes information over time, the Innovator's Scorecard gains accuracy. It is, after all, a snapshot of the imagined reality at any

---

7. But beware of earning a "Game Caution." See p. 311.

given point. The most valid picture is likely to be a sequence of several snapshots rather than any one single image.

Individual Bad Marks

No individual element score should be low enough to bar a venture. Low scores are simply a map of the land mines on the business's landscape. If you can disarm the mines, you may be able to succeed even if you have a low score. The lowest possible Showstoppers score applied to Orion, as discussed above. We were confronted by 130 angry nations allied against us in a functioning and legal cartel. We deserved a −10 on the Showstoppers score, which would have derived a −30 for the project. Was it fatal? Not at all—we succeeded! The point here is to persist and keep nurturing solutions to poor scores. They could some day bloom into respectable passing marks. The key to successful analysis using the Scorecard is the aggregate score. Can it reach at least a passing 70%?

Irrelevant Elements

From time to time you will be tempted to ignore an element or two. What, pray tell, could a famous person or a congressman have to do with your business idea? Plenty! I don't care if you are opening a commercial tool shed, if Tom Cruise loves your stuff, or if a congressman could stand guard over legislation that impacts tool sheds, you must pay attention. The moments that I have believed that an element was irrelevant were often followed by a revelation that I was being adversely impacted by an opponent on precisely that element. All the elements are here for a reason and you need to "squeeze your brain" to address each one honestly. There is, in my opinion, no such thing as an irrelevant element.

Reality

Be realistic. Intuitive estimates on a score are not excuses to be silly. Each one demands realism. One of the 44 elements indeed confronts the reality of the underlying business idea head on—see Pretending Not to Know on p. 261. A strength of this tool is its ability to derive practical results that are synchronized with reality across all of the elements.

Synthesizing the Scores

If you were to score a perfect 10 on all 44 elements, you would accumulate 860 total points. This is because the individual score on each element is multiplied by the weight or importance of each element. When you are ready to determine how you fared on the Scorecard, divide your total points by the maximum possible— 860. This is the score you need to use to determine if you should move forward. If you cannot reach a percentage close to 70, your idea really needs more work. Return to the elements that are below a 7 and improve those flunking scores until your aggregate exceeds 70%. If your score remains significantly below 70% even after you have twisted your idea and done all you can to improve the bad numbers, your idea could be in trouble.

Dr. Market's Observation:

It should be difficult to score below 70% if you have optimized your idea during the scoring process. Your idea is likely to have changed a little bit by the time you emerge from the scoring process so that it reconfigures itself into a passing score. Be as flexible as you can be and drive yourself into a situation that has a maximum chance for a successful launch. Don't be afraid to give up something about your idea if it can mean that you score higher and further assure yourself a big win. Also, don't forget to adjust all of the element scores to conform to the changes in your idea—if you change the idea halfway through the scoring, you need to start again from the top (it can't take long to redo the score!).

Overlap

Most of the scorecard elements slightly overlap other elements. You never know when you will catch a glimpse of a problem or a blessing that will have a material impact on the potential for success. If you believe that the product is sustainably unique but there is no way to confirm that the product is ahead of the market, there could be a problem. You may have stumbled onto a hidden competitor or product substitute, or even an ambush or something important that you were pretending not to know. Only after you score each item will you have a sense of the precise nature of the threat. Have patience.

Features of each item

Definition

Often the scorecard elements are idiomatic and where the dictionary is helpful in defining each term, we use it. Where we've used a phrase that you may not find in the dictionary, we will try to use common sense to explain what it means. This book uses the cultural lexicon of new venture launching. For example, while "showstoppers" and "low-hanging fruit" are not found in the dictionary just the way we require (showstopper here means something quite different from its dictionary meaning), the words themselves connote the appropriate image for our purposes.

Relevance—Why Add This Element?

Each element is described in terms of its relevance to a successful launch. In some cases there is relevance for the long-term prospects of the enterprise (see Strategy for Breaching the Chasm on p. 181). This section is in keeping with the learning process from which the Scorecard emerged. Learning can often bloom after a moment's reflection upon context and relevance and it is in this section of each element that I hope to explain why it is that the element has been added. If you don't understand the relevance, then you may not grasp why it is being addressed.

Where to find the answer?

Where can we find this information? Some of the information will be tough to unearth and some will be easy. In each case I will offer ideas about where you might quickly find a certain type of information. As time permits and with deeper research, the tool can become more accurate. But you need not dig deeply just now. Speed and nimble thinking are needed first, before we turn to facts and objectivity.

Score Elevation Tactics

How can we improve the score on this element? Unless the score is a 10, there is room for improvement on an element. I will suggest how to add points to the score directly, indirectly, or inferentially to improve the odds of launch success. Remember that the score must reflect reality. It is simply drawn from a different place on the analytical compass than objective research. If an item's score is low, we can drive it up in any legal way possible, including changing the law. This is where we consider how to make your idea simply perfect.

Practical Experience

How has this element worked in the past? This feature shares my personal experience and observations regarding the element. I hope my first-hand understanding of all the elements and their fit within the Scorecard helps you make the best assessment of your idea that you can. It is here that I hope to provide a well-grounded set of experiences to bring your understanding of that element into sharper focus.

Examples

How could this element look or feel if it materializes? This section offers some examples of what I believe is the essence of each element. Hopefully these observations will spark a thought or two as you launch your venture.

Putting the Number to the Scorecard

One surprising aspect of the Scorecard is the ease with which you can apply the scores. Let's try it a few times. What if we were trying to create a new broker–dealer securities firm that sells stocks and bonds? Compelling Unserved Need would absolutely deserve a negative score for element number one. It is so uncompelling that I would score it a –10. What about a cure for prostate cancer? If that is not a 10, it certainly deserves a 9 in the same element. How about the High-Profile Persons Available element for the new securities firm? Perhaps something positive, but until you contracted with someone special, it would have to remain in the low positives, say a 3. Win the support of Warren Buffet and you are into serious passing territory, say a 9 on that element. High-Profile Persons Available and the cure for prostate cancer? Same drill—I would score it a 3 (primarily because it surely should attract someone) unless you could win the support of a famous victim of the disease and then I would award it a 9 or a 10. As you can see, the scoring flows very easily and does not demand anxious precision. One thing to remember is that negative scores are reserved for crushing and penalizing scores and 7 or above is reserved for scores that pass and do not require much scrutiny in the future. You will be returning to the poorer scores to try to improve them. Just post the mark you feel it deserves on this element and move on. You will review each one several times before you tally your final aggregate score.

Part II

ELEMENTS OF
THE SCORECARD

DEMAND

Introduction

The elements have been organized into several groups to help you better understand the context and relevance of each one. We begin with Demand, and then proceed through Personal, Operations, Finance, Harvest, Daunting Negatives, The Story, and Carpe Diem. In this particular grouping relating to Demand, the 12 scorecard elements address the number one key strategic issue of any new venture, demand. Here we delve into the question, "Who cares?"

Why would your product or service make any difference and how will the market respond? However, remember that we are moving at light speed here, not opening a research project to sustain the production of a business plan. We are asking these questions quickly and up front. If the scores are not strong in the Demand group, there may be little need to move to the next.

Dr. Market's 30-Second MBA:

 All my classes, particularly the ones with really smart people like you, begin with a moment's communion with the notion of a going business. I call it the 30-Second MBA. What is a going business? Basically it is the creation, sale, and delivery of a product or service at high enough price to enough paying customers so that all the bills, including both fixed and unit, are paid with sufficient margin (profit) left over to provide the owners with an adequate return on their investment for having taken the risk in the first place. Keep this lesson in mind as you learn about the Innovator's Scorecard. As extra credit, you may wish to examine Appendix III on p. 321, where Dr. Joseph Schumpeter explains his famous observation about entrepreneurship being a "creative destruction."

Element 1

COMPELLING UNSERVED NEED

All men's gains are the fruit of venturing.
—Herodotus

Definition

Finding a compelling unserved need is a large piece of any matrix of success. It is also probably the easiest Scorecard element to understand. If your product fulfills a need, and that need is unserved elsewhere, and if it is compelling, then you could be well positioned for success. Of particular interest might be the intensity of the need, the flow of information that causes you to believe the need is unserved, and the inability of the average customer to work around the problem.

"Need"

A need is a lack of something required, desirable, or useful. It is a condition requiring supply or relief. However, unless the need is for air or relief from excruciating physical pain, there will be a question about the intensity of the need to the customer or market. Perhaps your best gauge of the intensity is the cost of the workaround or substitute. If no solution is quite right, and therefore there are several solutions at various prices, you may gain an advantage by offering one superior solution with one price.

"Flow of information"

Entrepreneurs who believe that they have found the Holy Grail of the "compelling unserved need" may be overlooking the fact that there is, indeed, a solution to that need already available. Most entrepreneurs with great new ideas are reluctant to discuss them with people who are in the best position to describe the competition. They do not wish to divulge the existence of their great idea, and so they refuse to communicate with people who could alert them to the presence of a cheap and effective substitute. There is no flow of information coming their way. If you find yourself cribbing or cheating here by forcing the recognition of need, you should assign yourself a lower score. Not to worry, you will have a chance to change it later.

"Work-arounds"

If the idea is revolutionary, such as the personal computer, there are not likely to be ways to describe the compelling need because the consuming public simply has no idea it needs the product. This raises the possibility of trouble elsewhere in the Scorecard, where scores on Closable Customers, Hot Market, and Cash Flowing

Now are all severely tested by a lack of zeal in the market. If the idea or product is not revolutionary, what are people doing today to solve the need served by this product? The value of your idea can soar when the features and benefits you can provide are being offered in the form of multiple products from several different vendors that consumers must aggregate to meet their needs.

"Compelling"

The best clue to the meaning of compelling comes from its root word, the Latin "pellere," to drive. With that as a cue, can you discern a "drive" to your identified need? Is there an automatic magnetism, energy, or top spin attracting a solution? Does your product alleviate pain, aggravation, or irritation? Look for a predisposition in the market to embrace, buy, or own your product. Will prospective customers leap at the chance to own some of your products? Why?

Relevance—Why Add This Element?

This could be the most succinct means by which to describe the anticipation of a successful new product—it fills a compelling unserved need. The relevance of the item is in its singular portrayal of the essence of success. It should be no mystery at all that if there is no need for your product, you have no business. If you cannot convince sufficient buyers that there is a compelling need for your product, hang up your spurs and try something else with your time. It is here that you need to return to your 30-Second MBA—if there is no compelling need, you will not sell enough products to pay your costs, let alone make a profit. So stop dreaming. Perhaps "critical" unserved need could be of sharper meaning, but for now "compelling" seems adequate to capture the spirit of the element.

It is possibly the most relevant of all the items to a predilection of success. This element represents the true essence or sine qua non of success. I don't want to press this too hard because it is so obvious. Much of what you will be considering with this Scorecard is the true nature of the need. If there is a need, is it compelling? If it is compelling, what makes you think so? If there is solid evidence of a compelling need, how many buyers will feel compelled to buy? And so on. It all starts here in this the most prominent of the elements.

Where to Find This Answer

Would a typical customer behave irrationally to own the product or receive the service before it existed as an offering by a company that does not yet exist? If the product or service were scarce, what premium would the customer be willing to pay? What savings could the product or service offer the customer? Fortunately, there are quick ways to identify the available substitutes. If there are adequate substitutes fully available at prices below yours, help me understand how compelling your product could be. In five minutes or so, Thomas Register, plus Google, Refdesk, and other search tools on the Web can offer names of companies who deliver products near to the one contemplated. (Search under a generic product or service name, or under the features and benefits you think the competition would offer.) Discovery of the compelling need is as simple as looking around the market for substitutes and competitors. If they are not visible, you could be onto something. Now you need to be able to explain why customers will crawl over broken glass to buy your product. What is so compelling about it that will drive people to own or use it?

Score Elevation Tactics

There are several ways to improve this score if you find yourself challenged. One ploy is to simply narrow the definition of the market. This improves the likelihood that you have a compelling unserved need. The problem of course is the likelihood that you will begin to pretend not to know that you have a significant substitute available. Another means to raise your score might be to collect evidence that your product fills a critical unserved need. In other words, simply reassure the public that your product or service fills the compelling and unserved need. This would consist of advertising, and it inspires the public to feel somehow deprived without owning or using what it is you have to offer. What advertising will you be using to boost awareness and an itch to own your stuff? Line up the priests—the gurus of the industry—and have them swear to the utility of this unique product. Rather than consume time, this can solve a number of questions simultaneously. For example, three renowned experts who swear that your product solves a compelling unserved need are also likely to carry with them skill sets and contacts worthy of participation in the enterprise. Naturally, there is a downside, in this case the potential for a claim of bias. These people will profit if you succeed because they have a stake in the game. One final maneuver might be to move the location to a place where the product truly would be compelling and unserved, such as overseas. See Quality of Evidence of Demand on p. 77.

Practical Experience—This Deserves the Maximum Weight of 3

No business launch can succeed without a passing score here. Quite often enterprises perform well when the need is *underserved,* yet served by a high-margin monopolist. This is where cost advantages can be helpful if not critical. As a reminder that this is a broad matrix of scores, fads can be forceful influences that should attract entrepreneurial zeal in the market. However, I am not aware of many fads that solved compelling unserved needs. The point is, if the score is low, don't give up just yet. Keep moving through the elements. See whether this element corrects itself after further thought. How is this possible? You could change the product into something that truly *is* needed in the market. This is what I was addressing earlier with the notion that the Scorecard can sometimes (often?) twist your product just enough to make it a big success. Just recognize that in the end, if no adjustment upward is possible, a failing score here is likely to doom your venture. My experience confirms that entrepreneurs are always alert to the changes required to succeed, so if changes seem necessary at this early moment, make them now.

If there is no compelling unserved need, it is my experience that you will be unable to establish and sustain your enterprise. You will be unable to spark sufficient imagination to attract support. How do you expect to succeed in a business with boring products in a market that is well served by others? Worse yet, how do you offer a product that is poorly defined in a place where there is no interest whatsoever or where repeated attempts with similar products have failed in the past?

The word "compelling" is often misunderstood by new entrepreneurs. They somehow fail to understand the distinction between "I have the cure for cancer" and "I have a new way to butter toast." Imagine the market and ask yourself whether your product will be something that, if it existed, would be simply irresistible.

Here in this first element in the Scorecard, we encounter the uncanny breadth and depth of the World Wide Web. If you use the Web for quick research on whether your idea is being offered elsewhere, in the blink of an eye you may find tens of thousands of "hits" demonstrating how compelling your product might or might not be. You have encountered your first dose of reality. Thank goodness there is no one watching your keystrokes to witness it.

Dr. Market's Observation:

 This is an appropriate moment to stop and think about another problem: confidentiality. The market has thieves who prey on creative genius. How do you dig around for clues about your idea's flight-worthiness and not give away the secret that is critical to your success? We have arrived at one of the many incongruities of launching new businesses. You must explore the market and "talk" to the experts but you need to keep things secret. One solution is to use this book to score your idea without talking to many (if any) other people. Another idea is to talk to only those who you can trust; make certain to ask them to keep it quiet. Yet another idea that I have used is to simply not give away the whole secret. Use a "what if" scenario and stay away from your true intentions. In the end, silence can be the best way to maintain confidentiality. Do not divulge the key aspects of your idea to anyone until you are prepared to seek investors and then you should try your best to not report 100% of what you are doing. If at this early moment in the life of your enterprise you have no legal protection, do not expose your secrets by letting them all out. In his book on commercial espionage, Boris Parad explains 79 different ways people can steal your business secrets.[1] This is where confidentiality agreements, crafted by your lawyers, will someday be helpful after your Scorecard earns a passing mark. But for the moment, please do not be naïve or you could lose it all before you start your engine.

---

1. *Commercial Espionage*, Global Connection Inc., 1997, ISBN 0-9658050-0-X.

Examples

Some of the possibilities for meeting compelling unserved needs include the following:

1. Cures for diseases.

2. Faster switching equipment in the nation's telecommunications infrastructure.

3. Shoes, tires, brakes, bushings, aircraft engines, and other heavy-use equipment that miraculously does not wear out.

4. Means of determining the presence of a nuclear threat.

5. Means to instantly divulge the precise location of the source of gunfire in an urban environment where guns are not allowed.

6. Techniques to fuse or repair torn spinal column or nerve connections such as the injury that felled actor Christopher Reeve.

The Coin-Operated Laundry—Compelling Unserved Need score: 5

Entrepreneurship is best tailored for taking an innovation to market, so it would be helpful to examine something that was both familiar to the average reader and blessed with an innovation. In each element we will take the Innovator's Scorecard on a test drive. Let's examine a hypothetical coin-operated laundry that will offer the services of machines that clean all materials and all stains. No stain will stand up to it. The machines are 25% more expensive than your competitor's machines, but properly set they will clean woolens and other fabrics that are otherwise extremely vulnerable to indelible stains. You also have the equipment necessary to clean and press suits and dresses and clean, starch, and press cotton shirts and blouses (although at lower and more traditional prices). The revenue model for the machine manufacturer is equipment sales and not a franchise based upon a patented process. The full scorecard for the Coin-Operated Laundry can be found in Appendix V. Regarding the coin-operated laundry's Compelling Unserved Need, I score it a 5. Clean clothes are always in style and the need for them is certainly compelling. However, we have a question on how well the market for clean clothes is served. Compelling? Sure. Need? Yes. Unserved? Hardly. The score here should reflect the highly competitive circumstances in the market. I would score this item, at least on the first round, at a 5. I would also expect to see the number improve after further consideration of the uniqueness of the cleaning, the ability to bottle up the availability of the product, and the circumstances surrounding the location of alternative cleaning establishments within that location.

> Element 1, Compelling Unserved Need *score summary:*
> Weight 3 x Score 5 = Total 15

Dr. Market's Observation

 Check out whether similar enterprises have been tried—and whether they were successful. For example, it might seem that a diner on a busy road would surely be successful. But, in Grand Forks, North Dakota, one such diner went through about eight iterations in 10 years, all with different owners, and all failed. It is now a tire dealership. Why did they fail? The location was almost impossible to reach by automobile. You could see it, but you "couldn't get there from here" because of the complicated traffic pattern and street layout. Whatever the need being served in that location, it was not compelling enough to lure people through an awkward intersection.

Element 2

EXPLAINABLE UNIQUENESS

When each thing is unique in itself, there can be no comparison made.
—D.H. (David Herbert) Lawrence, British author.

Definition

How unique is your product? Is it one of a kind, unequaled, and fundamentally different? Do the features and benefits fundamentally and profoundly differ from all others? In what way? Can the difference be explained or understood easily?

Relevance—Why Add This Item?

Products that are to be successful in the marketplace need to own some uniqueness, to be the only place where their particular features and benefits can be found. With uniqueness, a vibrant team of managers can build a genuinely valuable enterprise. Note that your uniqueness can be related to features of your product or service, the time it is offered, or the space or location in which it is offered. Will your product be the only one that delivers critical elements to customers who require them? If not, can it be the only product with those features that is available at a certain time and place? If there is no uniqueness, the business you hope to launch could be considerably more difficult to sustain. Please do not confuse uniqueness with the "unserved" aspect of the previous element. While there is similarity, that element deals with need and this deals with uniqueness.

Where to Find This Answer

This element is easy to miscalculate. Too often an idea will come to mind and no competition will be known, evident or acknowledged. However, upon discreet inquiry among knowledgeable sources you will see the substitutes and competitors bloom. You may be afraid to ask questions for fear that you could lead someone else to reach the same conclusions about the opportunity as you have. Trust, however, that your investors and their agents will all inquire about substitutes and competition. It pays to be informed about them.

Discovering competition often requires contacting sources who have no interest in competing, but whom you can trust and who are knowledgeable about the subject. Bear in mind that if you can both trust them and learn about the competition from them, they are likely to be among the best candidates for populating the venture either as members of the management team or on one of the boards. You must not and cannot keep your idea under a teacup.

Score Elevation Tactics

The best way to fortify your score here is to make certain that the features and benefits include a unique offering or two. It is often at this point that I implore my students to "squeeze their brains." Try harder. It is difficult to conjure up a new product that is devoid of uniqueness. So, use your brain as if the life of your little enterprise depended upon it. It is imperative that you find something unique about your product or else you must change your product slightly so that there truly *is* something unique about it. Remember when I told you that the Scorecard might deliver a business idea into your hands that is slightly different and much better than the first one? Here is one of the reasons. If you cannot uncover something unique, then you are almost certain to join those who will create stillborn enterprises. If all else fails, make your location unique, or if there is a sudden crisis, deliver your product at a critical time.

Practical Experience—This Deserves the Maximum Weight of 3

My experience with uniqueness suggests that what makes a new product or service unique is not always understood. Listeners reach quickly into their experience and conjure up a hasty response such as, "that's just like what Billy is offering down the street." Persist. Billy is more often than not completely disconnected from your market even though he once "thought about" doing something remotely similar but quite different. Persist and establish a uniquenesses that you can explain without surrendering many facts into a market full of sharks. Be as careful as possible while making certain that the listener clearly understands your product's uniquenesses.

Dr. Market's Observation:

 If you are lucky enough to have a lot of unique features and benefits, omit one or two of them from the list. Let the geniuses at the strategic investor or charter customer discover it on their own (maybe with a whisper to the CEO or managing partner who is always on the prowl for a way to show that they can come up with a great observation from time to time). Is this ethical? Paleeeeez! Of course it is, because it is exactly what people expect! Now then, in the fast and heady play of the game of launching a new enterprise, since there are sharks out there who systematically pillage the new enterprise field-of-play by lying, cheating, and stealing new ideas, no student of mine will spill all of the secrets in one data dump to try to win investors. Wake up! Keep some of the information in your pocket until later, because some of the people you approach will absolutely and certainly pass it along to your worst enemies. Trust and integrity are to be earned and established by both you and your investors.

Examples

Some possibilities for uniqueness include the following:

1. A patented drug that dramatically improves brainpower and memory enhancement. It is patented and one of a kind.

2. A true 3D color television receiver.

3. A means by which to re-use all frequencies used over the air today without interfering with existing users. This means that if channel 9 is for television, it can also be used at the same time for data.

4. Ownership of the only two-acre plot of land at the middle point of a 200-mile causeway over the ocean.

The Coin-Operated Laundry—Explainable Uniqueness score: 6

Clearly we know the capabilities of a cleaners and a coin-operated laundry. We also know the unique capabilities of this machine. However, the manufacturer of the machine is not franchising a patented process. They are selling machines and unless you can compel them to not sell to anyone else in your neighborhood, you will have no uniqueness. I score this as a 6. It is slightly more explainable than it is a compelling unserved need and it deserves one more point. However, it is still not a passing score. Score elevating tactics could include prevailing upon the manufacturer to divert the machines into a franchising system that would allow for acceleration of revenues and margins. It is only then that you would be able to explain the uniqueness and indicate that you owned that uniqueness in your neighborhood. You might also open a store for equipment and attempt to sell the equipment at a premium in your district.

> Element 2, Explainable Uniqueness *score summary:*
> Weight 3 x Score 6 = Total 18

Element 3

SUSTAINABLE DIFFERENTIATION

But the strong and healthy yeoman and husbands of the land,
the self-sustaining class of inventive and industrious
men, fear no competition or superiority. Come what
will, their faculty cannot be spared.
—Ralph Waldo Emerson, U.S. essayist, poet, philosopher.

Definition

We have examined uniqueness and its importance. Now for a more difficult part—keeping it. Can you *sustain* your uniqueness even under withering competition from inferior products? If you lose your uniqueness, can you regain it?

39

Relevance—Why Add This Element?

Uniqueness is a critical element of success. However, it can be fleeting in the face of a vigorous, competitive counteroffensive. If you cannot *sustain* the uniqueness, then you are certain to be confronted with questions about how you intend to protect yourself. Mediocrity or doom are certain to be your only possible destinations.

Where to Find This Answer

The answer to this question is sometimes more of a management process than anything else. Sagacious management will create a way to sustain the uniqueness. Yes, these things are not permanent and they have little to do with your product and a lot to do with you and your management team. A low score here can often be saved by clever tactics. Visibility of sustainability could be obscured in the early moments of a venture's development because, frankly, they have to do with the ability of the management to make certain that the features and benefits *remained* unique. That means that they will be on the prowl for goodies and trinkets that can be added to your product that no one can duplicate. Management prevents invasion of your uniqueness by competitors by making certain that your product remains unique.

Sustainability can imply legal monopoly such as a patent or trademark or it can be based upon a unique location such as a lonely street corner in the midst of federal parkland. It can also involve an exclusive relationship with resource vendors or distributors who themselves offer one-of-a-kind products or services. Note that as time goes on, uniqueness may diminish as substitutes and look-alikes begin to invade your territory. Patents, while helpful, are not foolproof protectors in the withering crosshairs of a good patent lawyer.

Score Elevation Tactics

If a log rests on top of a barn, sooner or later the log wins and the barn falls. If you stand there with an unimproved product, time and competition will outweigh your carefully crafted barn. Good management with a concerted drive to *sustain* the enterprise's uniquenesses should be able to prevail against the log, that is, the weight of competition, even if at first it appears that the uniqueness will fail. Careful hiring, partnering, or acquiring can all shore up a weak sustainability. However, just as certainly, if uniqueness cannot be sustained, you end up being the barn. Consider now what you will do to sustain your uniquenesses, including hiring, acquiring, and contracting. Here are some possible ways to elevate your score:

1. *Hiring* a former executive of a company with a similar mission (e.g., if you are in the business of supplying recycled newspaper to a paper mill, you might hire a former executive of an industry that knows and understands the paper pulp process).

2. *Partnering* with a like company that can broaden your offerings, extend your geographic reach, give you access to additional distribution facilities, or the like.

3. *Acquiring* a company that performs an integral or ancillary function (e.g., if you plan to open a chain of dry cleaning stores, you might consider purchasing a commercial laundry facility) or that tacks a new technology onto your set of offerings.

4. *Research* is often a key to sustaining your uniqueness because it is a constant search for revision or upgrades that would sustain your technological lead.

5. *Legislation* is sometimes used as a means by which to erect barriers to competition. See Government Relevance on p. 283,

which discusses government relations. Few things are more helpful in sustaining a uniqueness than an act of Congress.

6. *Litigation* is a tactic that is often used if you can catch your competitor doing something wrong, such as stealing employees (tortuous interference with an enforceable contract), stealing secrets (theft of protectable intellectual property), or infringing on patent/trademark/copyright.

Practical Experience—This Deserves the Minimum Weight of 1

Your ability to sustain a unique advantage could be the toughest element for a new venture to forecast. Once you go public with the idea, if it is compelling you can expect a surge of pretenders who hope to duplicate your feat. If you can own a unique piece of cyberspace (such as the name registry), indeed a piece of space itself (such as the one or two geosynchronous orbit slots from which telecommunications can stretch between the Mississippi and the Volga rivers), some uniquely valuable real estate, or some rare booty from which commercial value can be squeezed (such as a train set from the Orient Express), you can perform well here.

However, it is sometimes not realistic to forecast that you will be able to achieve effective sustainability. Patents often do not function as perfect defenses against replication. Appealing alternative locations in real estate can normally be substituted for the optimum spots. My experience is that claiming that your venture is guilty of not having a sustainable uniqueness is the typical excuse for prospective investors who "tank the deal" by somehow demolishing the possibility of your receiving cash from them if they are short of funds and want to back out. Honestly, they will never want you to know that they are out of money because that would harm their stature in the market. The truth is that in the long run, compelling products or services are not often sustainably unique. If you are rejected for funding for not being sustainably unique, you are likely to have lost the deal because of something else, perhaps a lack of funds, or possibly a politically incorrect matter such as your race, gender, age, or religion. Sustainability has little to do with uniqueness and very much to do with you and the management team. Let me move the dots a bit closer: if the investor declines to invest because your products are not sustainably unique, that rejection has little or nothing to do with the product or its uniqueness and a lot to do with something else, either their own embarrassment or something disquieting about your management.

Examples

Here are some possible examples of sustainable uniqueness:

1. Patent for the production of a critically useful pharmaceutical that is recognized by the FDA (note the double protection of the USPTO and the FDA). Here is one of those odd conundrums: do patents work or don't they? Investors and I believe that they are of limited utility. Why? Foreign intervention. Many countries that are robust in new technology development are reluctant to enforce global patents. So patents are therefore suitable only for casino odds. Sometimes you win and sometimes you lose. Good luck on predicting when and where.

2. Ownership and exhibition of the lost exhibits of the Baghdad Museum.

3. Ownership of the only bridge possible between two inhabited islands.

Dr. Market's Observation:

Businesses sometimes find ways to make it *appear* that they are sustaining their uniqueness. Don't be afraid to use a little poker bluff from time to time with a new feature or benefit that is interesting but not necessarily earthshaking. As in poker, however, don't get caught bluffing too often or someone will call you on it. New paint on your cab, a new menu at the restaurant, a name change on an ancillary product, a new software revision with only modest (and low cost) adjustments—these are all superficial yet potentially effective sustainers. From time to time, however, you will need to sustain your uniqueness with significant (and possibly costly) upgrades such as all-wheel-drive cabs, a new specialty chef, a new product instead of a name change, or a new piece of software from the bottom up. Do anything you can to keep your enterprise out in front of the game. The key here is relentless, energetic attention to distancing your enterprise from the competition at every opportunity. You snooze, you lose.

The Coin-Operated Laundry—Sustainable Differentiation score: 3

The differentiation here, while possibly real some day, could be quite unsustainable. I would score it a 3 just because it is better than nothing and roughly halfway to 50%, or 5. This is a serious flunk. If you wish, make it another number but not a 5 or above or a 0 or below.[1] To elevate this score you need to address the sustainability of your uniqueness. In the short term you could buy a machine, install it, and run your coin-operated laundry with it. However, in the long run, you could be overwhelmed with competition. How do you improve the score? Again, corner its availability in your establishment through a franchise. If this cannot be done, you are doomed to own a 3 here. Maybe less.

Element 3, Sustainable Differentiation *score summary:*
Weight 1 x Score 3 = Total 3

---

1. To award this a negative number, there would need to be some dreadful impact of the coin-operated laundry such as proof that you will be absolutely certain to violate the EPA rules against toxic waste.

Element 4

DEMONSTRABLE NOW

Is the concept demonstrable now or
does it need a feasibility stage?
—Call For Proposals, by the North West Science Review,
Government Office of the North West Manchester,
United Kingdom, 2000.

Definition

Quite simply, can the customer touch it, feel it, taste it, see it, sense it, or use it now? Even if the product or service is offered by a competitor, can anything like it be demonstrated now anywhere in the world?

Relevance—Why Add This Element?

This element monitors the end user's ability to understand the features, benefits, and value of the product or service you are planning to offer. It is a tricky element. The more demonstrable the product, the less likely that it has a sustainable uniqueness. By adding up substitutes customers might be able to gain the features and benefits of your product, though at much greater cost. You can still use the substitute product to demonstrate your own.

Perhaps the most important aspect of demonstrability is that it gives you a quick read on how quickly customers will grasp—and how highly they will value—the comparative advantages of your idea.

A low score here could mean that you will need to educate prospective buyers as to the features, benefits, and utility of the product. If significant public education is required on a product then the entrepreneur should plan on at least 10 years of lean times before break even, and even this could be an exceedingly brief estimate. The Internet was born in 1975 or so, the computer in the early 1950s, radio in the mid-1920s, television in 1940 or so, telephones in 1876, cellular phones in the mid-1970s unless you note the activities of the radio amateurs in the 1930's and 1940s (private conversations over two-way radios have been available commercially since WWII). In the case of products that have never seen the light of day before, the figure is at least 10, and probably is much longer. The point? It will take many years to reach break even if you are coming out with a product that is simply unknown to the mass of your target market.

Where to Find this Answer

Aside from the obvious case, in which a product is available for the customer to try, a certain amount of substitution is required to satisfy this element. This substitution can come from a competitor or from a firm that is delivering the closest substitute available. For completely new products, discoverability is easier with an analogy. "Think of a typewriter that corrects the errors, and stores a copy of your keystrokes." "Imagine a television attached to every possible database in existence." Naturally, much depends upon the source of your differentiation. Will it be price? Quality? Features?

Score Elevation Tactics

Can you build a prototype? Can you twist someone else's product with an attachment? Can you build a video or animation with enhancements from another firm's product? Can you do a better job of explaining the distinction between what you ultimately will provide and the features and benefits of what can already be placed into the consumer's hands? Can you convince customers that a purchase will fulfill their expectations?

Practical Experience—This Deserves the Minimum Weight of 1

Customer confidence can be hard to win if you have a product that defies easy understanding. At PTAT we were attempting to actually sell pieces of an undersea fiber optic cable to the end users[1]. Until that time they were aware only that their circuits terminated overseas and any sophisticated knowledge or understanding was therefore unnecessary. But a new era in telecommunications began when customers could actually own their own portion of the pipe in

---

1. For further explanation see Appendix II.

a condo arrangement. People had trouble understanding this when we pitched the sale. So we handed out actual one-inch-long pieces of the cable along with an explanation of its physical path, including a survey of all the wrecks at sea between New York and England. We had been able to determine that the cable we were selling passed very close to the Titanic and several other interesting wrecks. Armed with the map and a section of the cable, we received 17 preliminary expressions of interest in the purchase of capacity on our cable more than 17 months before it was installed and placed into service. Seeing and touching pieces of the actual cable, as well as understanding its projected whereabouts, made all the difference.

Dr. Market's Observation:

 Use plenty of metaphors if you cannot provide a working copy. The point is to make the prospect comfortable with what it is you are selling. For a really revolutionary idea, the substitution can even come from your imagination. Consider this early description of television: "radio with pictures."

Examples

Whatever your imagined product or service, can you

- touch it,

- smell it, or

- use it or something similar to it today?

The Coin-Operated Laundry— Demonstrable Now score: 8

Clearly this deserves a solid passing score. Your competition is offering coin-operated laundry services and no one is confused about what might be offered. While your score on Compelling Unserved Need was low, here there is no doubt about the utility of your product. People know how to use the substitute and they use it often. However, there is the added feature of being able to clean everything. I would score it an 8 and when the machine is available in your facility naturally it would score a 10. The point is sufficient familiarity of the public for them to understand and embrace your product with the new and compelling features in a hurry.

> Element 4, Demonstrable Now *score summary:*
> Weight 1 x Score 8 = Total 8

Element 5

GOOD COMPETITION

A man comes to measure his greatness by the regrets, envies and hatreds of his competitors.
—Ralph Waldo Emerson

Definition

In an entrepreneurial game, the last thing we want to see in our space is a competitor. They leach off market share, they disrupt any marketing momentum, they have expertise, they own brand awareness, they have representation in the legal community, and so on. What possible good could come from a competitor of any shape or size? For one thing they could be doing an appalling job, one that could not possibly withstand the onslaught of a determined market intruder. They might be huge, and they might be a 130-nation international cartel. Their prices could be 10 times higher than domestic rates using the identical technology and their service could beg for investigations into fraud. They could be irreversibly terrible at the game of business and they could be simply heading for oblivion—they could be walking around bankrupt, not paying their bills, or in some other way not managing their business well. What are they "good" for? Teaching your prospects how important *your* products will be to them because *your* products will not let them down. I'm tempted to say that they are not merely "good," they're great!

Relevance—Why Add This Element?

Even a weak competitor can confirm that there are customers willing to pay for your product or service. Your prospective customers are likely to understand very well how your product or service behaves. However, note that your competitor may also be offering features and benefits that are inferior to yours and when you arrive, you could confirm the market wisdom of your product and attract a competitor who attempts to sneak up on you in the market and steal your customers (I call this an ambush; we talk about it on p. 89). Like a chameleon, they could change from good to bad overnight. Good competitors exist often but their reactions must also be anticipated. You must calculate now, up front, if these people are capable of turning on you and obliterating your ability to seize market share.

Perhaps most importantly, if properly timed and powered, your marketing campaign could result in an abrupt and irreversible market shift toward your product and away from theirs. Remember, they are "good" because they are so bad. They are essentially incompetent, or at least incapable of managing their business in the space you hope to conquer. Customers who feel cheated by your "good" competitors have a reservoir of demand for your competing product or service that works well for you. You must be able to serve all of them quickly to exploit the situation. And don't forget to bring long-term agreements for them to sign. This will prevent their migration back to the competition.

A weak competitor might be having difficulties that could someday apply to you. It is worth noting and exploring the reason, particularly before you launch. The more significant and relevant the competitor's source of trouble to you, the lower your score on this item.

Dr. Market's Observation:

Keep in mind one consequence of your weak competitor's filing for bankruptcy protection under Chapter 11: For some substantial period of time they will be playing the game with low to no costs. While under the protection of the law, the court will allow them to compete without paying their bills.

Where to Find This Answer

You can find weak competitors by spotting elevated levels of complaints from customers in Better Business Bureau records and in the tort cases in the county where they are headquartered. They can be found in the archives of the local newspaper available on the Web, often at no cost. Is this a regulated industry, and if so, what does the regulator say? Is there a friendly legislator who can champion your cause for you in that regulated industry (don't forget to anticipate an indication that a solid campaign contribution would be a smart thing to do[wink wink]).[1] It can also be helpful to know which competitors are in financial, public relations, or legal difficulties, and why—these are all things that should certainly be open and notorious. In-depth, time-consuming research is not necessary for your preliminary score.

Score Elevation Tactics

If the source of the competitor's weakness is poor management or a self-defeating culture, then you can improve your score. Conjure up the most likely strategic plan for the competitor and measure their performance against it. Note however that time is of the essence. You will need to use opinion and intuition rather than fact and research. Quickly forecast what the unbiased experts would say had they had the time to research and respond. If this is not possible, find someone you know and trust who understands the business.

Practical Experience—This Deserves the Medium Weight of 2

An arrogant competitor may also be weak, because management is not paying attention to the business. They are not running their business as if they had customers who could go elsewhere. Are they bluffing? Do your homework. Watch. Listen. Think. Post your

---

1. This was a huge surprise when Orion Satellite sought the assistance of a famous senator in 1983—there was a price to pay for his support and he asked for the money. Honest.

score now based on your hunch. Realize that this score will change in unpredictable ways when they become aware of your intentions.

Examples

Here are some examples of how "good competition" looks or feels:

1. Old-line commercial airline service between high-traffic city pairs (somehow JetBlue Airways and Southwest Air have discovered how to do this right, in the face of "good" competition from American, United, Continental, Delta, etc.).

2. Taxi service in Washington, DC (at least the price is right, but there is little oversight over vehicular safety and cleanliness).

3. Local telephone service in rural America. (Note the cautionary word above about the frailty of the underlying idea rather than the poor management of the competitor. In other words, a "good" competitor could be in a business in which no one can succeed. This is one of those elements that makes a lucid and powerful point about the potential for success in your chosen market.).

Dr. Market's Observation:

Yes, you should consider the possibility that a prospective competitor is "good" because the market or the business is terrible, not the competitor. However, those circumstances are amply covered by other elements of the Scorecard that deal with demand, resources, distribution, and funding. For this element, focus upon whether there is someone who is attempting to serve your customers who is "good" because he or she is so bad at their business.

The Coin-Operated Laundry—
Good Competition score: 10

There are certain to be many people out there who are demonstrating the worthiness of launching a business in this space—the laundry business. This item scores a perfect 10 because none of them have the ability to offer cleaning services that are guaranteed by technological innovation to be perfect. In other words, all your competitors are serving your customers with an inferior product. All you need to do is promote, process, and deliver.

> Element 5, Good Competition *score summary:*
> Weight 2 x Score 10 = Total 20

Element 6

BAD COMPETITION

*Competition is the keen cutting edge of business,
always shaving away at costs.*
—Henry Ford

Definition

Competition in the context of new enterprises is normally a problem
(however, don't forget the discussion of "good" competition above).
In this case, competition is from a firm with robust resources, solid
talent, a penchant for quality strategic management, excellent
products, and a large and adoring clientele. This would be the
quintessential "bad" competitor, that is, a person or enterprise who
will simply devour your customers because they are truly gifted and
blessed in running the business against which you are attempting to
compete with your precious resources.

Relevance—Why Add This Item?

In every sense of the word, this competition is "bad." It means that your success must come at the expense of an enterprise that has the resources, including a robust core competence (highly skilled work force and well-oriented organization), to hamper your successful launch. Sadly, many new entrepreneurs believe they have no competition when in truth they do. Note however that if you have some critical "unfair" advantages,[1] particularly if a federal license is involved, it can make you stronger than your competition. It could pay dividends to be persistent and keep grooming and toying with your idea until it reaches a passing score.

The implications of a strong competitor can be profound. Your customer base is in doubt, your vendors can be unreliable, the cost of capital can be elevated, distribution can be spotty, the best law firms and advisors can be on the competitor's payroll so that they cannot work for you, seed capital can vanish, and the risks can be elevated. This could be a formula for doom.

Where to Find This Answer

To find your score here, examine the market for competent competition. What are people doing today to substitute for your product? If several different products are necessary to provide the same feature and benefit package delivered by your product, you may have a chance because of convenience, single integrated sourcing, and possible cost advantages.

---

1. This is not a hall pass for you to do something evil or unethical. "Unfair" will be the term used by your opponent when they cannot do much about the advantage you have created. They will whine about it being unfair. It is so important that it is the subject of Element 32 and is weighted the max, a 3.

Score Elevation Tactics

If you score low here, learn more about your customers' requirements and their match to the features and benefits of your competitor's product. Can you make the case that the competitor is somehow failing to serve the requirements of the customer? Is the competitor willing to make the required changes so as to become a devastating "bad" competitor? Will any investor believe you? Can you carve a niche with ample and cost-effective customer service? Do you have some inside track to the customers and or their suppliers or distributors? Is there a legal barrier that you can exploit? Are your "unfair" advantages adequate to trump any advantage held by the competitor? Is there any way to co-opt the competitor into using your product?

Dr. Market's Observation:

Remember that one of the jobs of the Scorecard is to force you to twist your idea into the maximum possible potential for success. If this means becoming a vendor to what otherwise could be a competitor, you might stand a better chance of succeeding.

Practical Experience—This Deserves the Maximum weight of 3

Unless you have a significant advantage that you can deliver (for example, if you own a cost structure about 10% of those of the bad competitor), you need to pause just now to reconfirm the wisdom of what you are doing. If there is direct head-to-head competition in the market, it could be smart for you to back off and change your idea slightly to find the open path to success. The Military Network was an attempt to relaunch the bankrupt Military Channel. Aside from the taboos in airing a channel devoted to the military[2] and the yawning problems associated with raising the money (roughly $100 million for starters), nothing prepared us for the competition waiting for us after 9/11. Suddenly, six major networks were carrying our material and serving our customers with distribution assured to all 80 million homes in America. Despite the fact that we would still be the only channel devoted to the military, we suddenly had no chance of success. In the end, if bad competition exists, back away from the opportunity (remember, it is still just an idea) and do something else with your idea. Make the changes necessary to succeed.

Examples

Here are some examples of strong competition:

1. Local supermarket in the neighborhood where you are considering a butcher shop.

2. Subway under a river on which you are considering the establishment of a privately owned ferry.

3. Microsoft when you are considering the creation and marketing of a new operating system.

---

2. Investors and advertisers often eschew channels that aggrandize the use of a war machine to solve diplomatic problems. They are basically pacifists, even though your shows might frequently be found on their home televisions.

The Coin-Operated Laundry—
Bad Competition score: 0

This element is trouble. There are certain to be cleaners in your community who dwell upon extraordinary service and who "own" your customers. These are very "bad" people as far as you are concerned and your score here is a 0. Improving this score will involve a vigorous promotion of your uniqueness so that the "bad" competitors convert into "good" competitors who deliver inferior service. However, if there are one or two firms that are well established, well capitalized, and well run, it will be difficult to keep them away from the technology that renders your service so superior. These bad competitors could remain "bad" if they are run by good business managers. This score on this element is particularly troublesome.

> Element 6, Bad Competition *score summary:*
> Weight 3 x Score 0 = Total 0

Element 7

COMPELLING PRICING POSSIBLE

Cheapness: Low price, bargain, drug in the market.
—Mawson, C.O.S., ed. *Roget's International Thesaurus*, 1922.

Definition

One enchanting propellant for your success could be the possibility of cost savings for your customers. It could fuel demand better than any other benefit, *assuming* you have comparable quality. If customers were to purchase your product, is there any possible argument that doing so will create considerable savings for them? Note that the pricing advantage should be sustainable unless there are extraordinary features whose benefits overwhelm the need for a premium or low price. Or, from a slightly different perspective, can you win market share temporarily by selling at or below cost for an introductory period?

65

Relevance—Why Add This Element?

Price can be compelling if customers will indeed enjoy substantial savings over the cost of current substitutes. Note that if competitors fear low-priced intruders like you, they could react defensively by trying to secure their customers with long-term buying commitments. The bottom line is that cost savings will drive the market in your direction and could be a good reason to move the launch smartly to a successful dawn. Carpe diem.[1]

Where to Find This Answer

Compare your expected unit *costs* with the *price* of the competitor's product. If you can foresee that your costs will be significantly lower than the offering price of your competitor, perhaps you have an advantage. Naturally you cannot know for certain until you have actually calculated your unit costs including all variable and fixed. Note too that it is the ancillaries market where this element can be quite vivid. Watch for savings in these

---

Dr. Market's Observation:

 This is yet another area where a competent and aggressive management team will earn its keep for investors. They will want to know whether you and your team can hold down costs so that the market flows naturally in your direction with plenty of margins to make this opportunity worth the investment risk.

---

1. Latin for "sieze the day" or move quickly.

closely associated ancillary products or services such as insurance, warehousing, distribution, or other costs required to twist existing substitutes into compliance with the compelling needs of the customer. If your product does not need these expensive add-ons, you could have a significant advantage worth touting now. For example, your pricing could become compelling if you could deliver motion pictures without installing the expensive wires necessary to deliver cable TV to the home.

Score Elevation Tactics

To elevate a poor score, streamline the production and delivery of your product now, up front, in nontraditional ways. Examine the distribution patterns of the substitutes. Research the ancillary products required to satisfy fully the customers' needs. If you are selling trailers, does there need to be a vehicle for pulling the trailer? Does it make sense to build trucks to pull them? Can the ancillary products be intertwined in your product mix? Can you afford an introductory price that tends to preempt the market?[2]

Practical Experience—This Deserves the Minimum Weight of 1

Your early customers will likely demand low prices because they are uncertain whether your products will be delivered, whether

---

2. This is one of the luxurious moments of entrepreneurship. As you gain a solid understanding of the new business or industry, costs that are sacred cows of the industry will fall out because you are not stuck with honoring them. You can employ dramatic shortcuts in your production or operational processes that do not sacrifice quality. Southwest Air and JetBlue qualify for the Compelling Pricing Hall of Fame.

they will be supported, and whether they will be reliable. Some might request stock warrants because they would be taking a chance on you and they realize they have you "over a barrel." So it is difficult to say no to these up-front demands.[3] The key is, can you afford it? In any event you should mount a spirited defense of your pricing and its margins. Bottom line? Never ever turn away your first customer. Take the deal at whatever cost and run to the market with the news: you are in business!

Examples

Here are a couple of possible examples:

1. Sell two for the price of one, limited time only.

2. Give away samples, but only if the cost is not prohibitive.

3. Free trial if you are offering a service.

4. Piggybacking or packaging with key resource or distribution channel.

The Coin-Operated Laundry—Compelling Pricing Possible score: 0

By our assumption, the cost of our equipment is 25% higher than that of our competitors. Compelling pricing is therefore

---

3. Actually, you might be able to use the leverage of being able to call your biggest customer an "owner." Waring Partridge of AT&T Strategic Planning fame once used this ploy as a matter of practice, delivering occasional bonanzas to AT&T while rewarding the new vendors with the ability to say " . . . we are owned in part by AT&T." Over the years, Waring contributed far more to AT&T than his compensation cost them, just by being clever and asking for a few shares to sweeten the deals with new vendors. AT&T was these vendors' first customer.

questionable. Until more evidence arrives, it must score a 0. Improving this score will involve a careful calculation of how many clothes are ruined each year by traditional cleaners because of their inferior technology. If you can calculate that number and then promote it unmercifully, you could significantly elevate this score.

Element 7, Compelling Pricing Possible *score summary:*
Weight 1 x Score 0 = Total 0

Element 8

CLOSABLE CUSTOMERS

When I see a merchant over-polite to his customers, begging them to taste a little brandy and throwing half his goods on the counter—thinks I, that man has an axe to grind.
—Charles Miner, from "Essays from the Desk of Poor Robert the Scribe," Doylestown, Pa., 1815. It first appeared in the *Wilkesbarre Gleaner*, 1811.

Definition

Can you "see" your customers? Do you know how many exist, at least in rough terms? Do you know their names or how to find them? Can you forecast where added customers are hidden if the enterprise needs to grow dramatically? Can you adequately articulate your vision to them? Can you forecast how much they will buy? Now for the killer—can you close a deal with any of them right now, long before you have written your business plan?

Relevance—Why Add This Element?

Customers need to buy your products in sufficient quantity and at a high enough price to cover all your costs, fixed and marginal (remember Dr. Market's 30-Second MBA?). Even if it is impossible to predict who might be interested in these products or services up front, the business still may never materialize. There is only one way to test your idea—sell someone on your products today, and I mean right now. The "axe to grind," referred to in the Miner quote above, is the validation of your product. If you can sell it now you are likely to be onto something, possibly something big.

Where to Find This Answer

The Scorecard is a preliminary and intuitive scoring matrix. Therefore, make your best guess about what your sales prospects would be if you were to shine your shoes, put on a suit, go into the big daunting market, and try to close a sale. What would happen? Who would you expect to absolutely, positively buy your stuff?

Score Elevation Tactics

If this score is low, pick up the telephone. Talk to some prospective customers. Inquire of the market. Determine if you can state the case in a succinct manner, from the heart while you look them in the eye. Can you create a user group? Can you afford to issue some stock warrants to charter customers? There are few effective substitutes for direct contact with the market. Trust that any professional investor will reach out to the customer community to weigh the depth of demand before they allow their enthusiasm to bloom. Save him or her the trouble and attach a purchase contract[1] or two to your presentation panels.

Dr. Market's Observation:

While attaching shares of stock to the very earliest of customers, particularly big ones, can be a useful tactic, please be very careful about how much equity you spend to kick start your business. If cash is king, then equity is queen. Treat your shares as if they were the crown jewels because someday you will be selling them. The point is that if you do not spend your cash and equity wisely, you may not be able to make the business a success.

Practical Experience—This Deserves the Medium Weight of 2

Can you close a sale today for a product that does not exist, owned by a company that has not yet been organized? Will you be able to write the first edition of your business plan with several customer contracts in the appendices? If not, you should be wary about your prospects for success. My pre–business-plan experience has been full of surprises. It seems that when I expect to close a sale early, something causes delay. Other times the sale closes quickly, because the customer has a critical need for the products.

Orion and PTAT both were able to attract customers before they existed, and in most classes I have taught over the past seven years we have had winners of my Champagne Award[2] for this seem-

---

1. Or written expressions of interest or best of all, their checks. Don't laugh—it actually happens.

ingly impossible feat. The first one was at the University of Maryland, where a team arrived in class one day with a $16,000 check from Hewlett-Packard for the first copy of a Y2K software package that had been developed by the team's engineers in China. Perhaps the biggest catch was the commitment made by NYNEX, Oxford Health, Barr Labs, and others for a telemedicine product developed by a team at Columbia University—$5 million—at a meeting organized by a team of brilliant MBA candidates who secured the commitment before they had written their business plan.

Examples

Here are some possibilities:

1. Fleet contract with the police department if you are building a car wash.

2. Restaurant table linen cleaning contract if you are preparing to create a cleaners or laundry.

3. Hotel builder contract for a furniture store.

The Coin-Operated Laundry— Closable Customers score: 10

This is clearly a high-scoring element. There are plenty of people who will insist on the very finest cleaning and you will certainly do business with them. This element deserves a 10. If it were somehow low, we would immediately invade the high-use commercial

---

2. I provide a bottle of real French champagne (unless another fluid would be more appropriate) to each team member of the first team to arrive in class with cash from a customer prior to the publication of their business plan.

establishments and strike deals that would ensure our extended survival. Restaurants, hotels, police departments (uniforms), and hospitals would all be contacted for special long-term arrangements. The next question is sufficiency of numbers.

Element 8, Closable Customers *score summary:*
Weight 2 x Score 10 = Total 20

Element 9

QUALITY OF EVIDENCE
OF DEMAND

Evidence: 1. The evidence or argument that compels the mind to accept an assertion as true...Convincing or persuasive demonstration: was asked for proof of his identity; an employment history that was proof of her dependability.
—The American Heritage Dictionary of the English Language, fourth edition, 2000.

Definition

Quality of Evidence of Demand measures the strength of your belief that there is a market. Is it a hunch? What substantiates your guess? Did a primary vendor lose its warehouse to fire? Did a purchasing officer just whine about the lack of vendors of your product? How many experts will swear that the demand level you sense out there is valid? Is there some recorded indication of demand? Why do you believe that anyone would buy your stuff?

Relevance—Why Add This Element?

At some point in the progression from idea to market, the product must have an encounter with demand. The question we're asking here is how certain you are that customers will be waiting for your products. The higher the score the easier it will be to attract critical resources including personnel and capital.

Where to Find This Answer

Add any evidence you have that is more concrete than a hunch or whim. If your evidence is a whim, you score low. If it is concrete such as written and signed expressions of interest from customers, or a protective charter or contract, you score high. Why is it that you are convinced there is demand? It is possible that the evidence of demand was the spark that ignited the idea in the first place. It is also possible that the first evidence was just a hunch. Discovering this element involves little more than inquiring of yourself, "How do I know?"

Score Elevation Tactics

Letters or e-mails from prospective customers or unaffiliated experts, petitions, conditional contracts, and polls are excellent ways to improve this score. It is worth inquiring of a couple of people what they would do if your product were offered. Get their answers in writing.

Practical Experience—This Deserves the Medium Weight of 2

Perhaps a bit of news, information, or complaint you heard is what first indicated demand before your idea was born. You can judge the quality of this evidence by the origin and number of the complaints, the purchasing power of the complainant, and the estimated cost and difficulties involved in delivering your products. Entrepreneurs, and particularly serial or repeat entrepreneurs, are quite gifted at spotting this evidence and allowing it to drive a quick analysis of whether it's worth the effort to pursue the idea.

Dr. Market's Observation:

If you saw high-quality evidence of demand, trust that others saw it too. Be prepared to move fast. And for goodness sake, collect all the evidence so you can prove your case for demand to your investors!

Examples

Here are some ways to confirm evidence of demand:

1. Newspaper articles that cite the source. Confirm the facts by calling the source.

2. Court documents whose authenticity and accuracy are some-what guaranteed.

3. Letters or other written expressions of interest including e-mail—the key is having a written record and being able to authenticate it.

The Coin-Operated Laundry—Quality of Evidence of Demand score: 5

There is plenty of evidence of demand for cleaning services. Unfortunately, other than conjecture, there is no evidence that services with guaranteed results would be worth the extra fees. The score on this element can't be in the passing range, although it should be positive. I am awarding it a 5. Elevating this score will involve working carefully with the manufacturer to understand their hard numbers for demand. It would also be prudent to understand the nature of damages done to clothing by routine cleaning services. These will all allow a higher score to be awarded.

> Element 9, Quality of Evidence of Demand *score summary:*
> Weight 2 x Score 5 = Total 10

Element 10

AHEAD OF THE MARKET

Nothing is so corrupting as a great idea whose time is past.
—John P. Grier

Definition

Ask yourself whether you will be ahead of the market—that is, will your product or service arrive in the market at just the right moment to capture more than your fair market share? Timing, velocity, and direction of an opportunity are important. Think of skeet or trap shooting. After taking into consideration the trajectory, direction, changes in altitude, wind (demand), velocity of the clay pigeon, and the characteristics of your weapon (your product), can you lead the target (your market) so that your shot (the delivery of your product) meets it at just the right moment?

81

Velocity, direction, wind, and change in altitude

Can you spot the flight characteristics of the market? How fast are things changing? In what direction is the market headed? Is it curving or steady? Is it changing altitude or strength? How quickly can you determine the answers to these questions (your answer should be in minutes rather than days)?

Mass and muzzle velocity[1]

How difficult is your product to design, produce, and deliver? How fast can your product travel to the market? How far can it travel before it falls to earth? What flight pattern does your product need to follow to intersect with a customer? Do you have the capital resources needed to hit the target with sufficient mass?

Muzzle swing (tricks you can use)

Obviously you are not likely to be using a swinging muzzle. A more apt metaphor might be "radar-guided muzzle swing." Can you lock up a large number of customers in one contract, say, with a trade association? Can you turn expressions of interest from a sizeable portion of your customers into a handsome deposit of earnest money before you seek your capital? How about a letter of credit conditional upon satisfactory delivery?

---

1. This is a centuries-old term relating to the operational characteristics of a gun or cannon. How fast does the bullet exit the end of the tube? It is a function of the powder in the charge, the mass of the bullet, the presence of rifling used for accuracy, etc. The metaphor is useful here because of the need to aim and fire the weapon ahead of the target as it moves through the marketplace. The "bullet," or product, arrives at the target at just the right time to capture market share and succeed.

Relevance—Why Add This Element?

It is difficult to gauge demand and production so as to arrive on the scene just ahead of the market, but if you think you can do it, your score should be high. Timing, speed, exclusivity, vision, confidence, and all those qualities that people call luck will come into play. Frankly, luck is nothing more or less than doing something at just the right time in just the right direction that no one else anticipated. Then market demand matches the arrival of your product in such a way as to lift sales revenues quicker than would otherwise be possible.

Where to Find This Answer

Remember that you are using an intuitive tool that helps you gauge your lead on the market.

Product Demand

- Can you sense how fast things that will have a material impact upon the consumption of your products are changing?

  - Is there a population bubble on the horizon? For example, are more customers about to want your product because it is targeted to a special need of the Gen Y or baby boomer population?

  - Have there been any advances in underlying technology (e.g., computer chip speeds, metallurgy, fiber optic efficiencies, etc.) that will help you get to market faster?

  - Have there been changes in the law that will now allow greater efficiencies to occur?

- Are there penalties for the customers who therefore must continue to rely upon the old products?

- Can you offer your product or service in a geographic market that does not yet have access to it? This is where the market demand has clearly not yet arrived—you will be able to fire your product at that market before the demand hits.

- In what direction is the broadly defined market for your type of product headed?

  - Is it on a steady rise?

- Is the market changing altitude or strength?

  - What is the reason for the change?

    - Customer needs and tastes?

    - Increase/decrease in level of customer satisfaction with existing products or services?

    - External reasons, such as the state of the economy?

Speed to Market

- What is the pace of change in the products required by the customers?

- How difficult is it to design, produce, and deliver your product?

- How long will it take?

- How long will your lead last?

- Are you able to solve a critical distribution issue as the primary product arrives on the market? In other words, can you deliver your product a little quicker so that it arrives in a more timely fashion?

Score Elevation Tactics

The first challenge is to calibrate your lead on the target market with the timing of your delivery. In logical progression, here are the key questions:

- Can you define your target market, particularly its motion and scale?

- What is about to happen in the market that could directly affect demand for your product?

- How well suited is your product to their anticipated needs?

- Are you better suited for a different market, that is, if your product fails to lead your target market, what market *does* it lead?

- What are the technological innovations that are about to emerge?

- Can your products complement the new innovations?

- Thinking geographically, can you be the first to deliver these products or services in remote cities?

- Can you lead the market in some other country?

- Can you create a contract or expression of interest that could lock you into your success? This method of locking your product onto a moving market is the easiest to understand— it's a bit like radar guidance of your product's delivery to the arms of the customer at just the right time.

Practical Experience—This Deserves the Medium Weight of 2

Few things are more predictable than the success of a well-timed and well-aimed "shot" at a bubble of demand that is moving through the market. Yes, you can miscalculate the lead on your market and you can misapply your resources. However, if you are an able and decisive manager with ample leadership skills and potent and mobile resources that can hit the sweet spot of demand on the fly, you can create a legend of yourself, not to mention an exemplary net worth.

Examples

Here are some possible examples of leading the market:

1. Wheelchair manufacturing as the baby boomer generation nears retirement.

2. Bus service to the location of a soon-to-be-opened casino.

3. Artfully manufacturing and selling T-shirts for an upcoming championship football game the instant the two opponents are named.

4. Soliciting the purchase of gold and defense stocks the instant America is attacked.

The Coin-Operated Laundry—Ahead of the Market score: 5

Obviously, you are not ahead of the market for cleaning clothing. However, there could be a cultural or population trend worth noting. Are people cleaning their clothing more or less? Is the population growing or shrinking? Are fabrics becoming more or less delicate? Do people wear suits and dresses more or less? A quick, instinctive check suggests that people are not changing their cleaning habits much but that they are at a low in wearing suits and dresses. This could be changing if there is continued evidence that more and more people are dressing up for work. Fabrics are improving in their defenses against stains, not a good thing for this enterprise. The score for this element is 5 because people will use the service but the element needs to be improved with added market information regarding cultural and business trends. One promising note is the possibility that people are indeed dressing up more for work. This could easily be the leading edge of a swing back to a touch more formality in the work place, a trend that will serve this business well.

Element 10, Ahead of the Market *score summary:*
Weight 2 x Score 5 = Total 10

Element 11

AMBUSH EXPOSURE

*War is not a life: it is a situation, One which
may neither be ignored nor accepted,
A problem to be met with ambush and
stratagem,Enveloped or scattered.*
—T.S. (Thomas Stearns) Eliot, U.S.-born—British poet, critic.

Definition

Ambush Exposure is the possibility that some invisible "competitor" with extraordinary means and resources could find your product or service so compelling or threatening that they plunge into your market and help themselves to your customers. Likely ambushers are often somewhere in your value chain, such as resource vendors or distributors who are expanding horizontally into your space. Ambush is a particularly effective tactic in matters involving government purchasing because the people inside the government are notoriously "leaky" when it comes to information

89

and procurement management. The winners in this game are
rarely surprised.

Relevance—Why Add This Element?

Being ambushed is a bit scary. If you can anticipate an ambush, you
are forewarned about potential trouble. If you fail to anticipate and
an effective ambush is carried out, you can lose it all. A touch of
paranoia can be a good thing.

Where to Find This Answer

These sleeping dogs have unallocated resources that could quickly and
quietly produce substitutes for your products. Who would suffer the
most from your success? Whose business would your creativity harm?
Buggy whips and impact typewriters were victims of ambushers—
they "owned" the customers that automobiles and computers now
serve so well. It remains to be seen whether POTS (plain old telephone
service with its switches and twisted pairs) and newspapers will
succumb to IP (Internet protocol) and electronic media. Another
approach is for you to determine who uses your distribution networks
and who uses your vendors for other products. Who in your value
chain has resources or products that they could easily fashion into a
head-to-head confrontation with you in the market?

Score Elevation Tactics

There are a number of ways to avoid an ambush. The best way, of
course, is to create a product whose uniquenesses are plentiful and
sustainable to preempt those who might consider competing with

you. Another tactic is to examine the management practices of the potential ambusher. Gauge their cunning in market circumstances such as this. How sleepy are they? How pernicious? Make your case and proceed, or not. You may prefer to remain hidden until a certain critical mass in the market has been achieved or assured. You may also consider instituting a blocking maneuver of some form (such as with a critical resource vendor or distributor) that would prevent competitors from moving against you.

Another ploy is raw deception—there is no law that says you cannot engage in a market feint. Do not divulge your true intentions until the market is solidly behind you. You might also manipulate the timing. If they have an event or product roll-out, time your announcement to coincide roughly with theirs—steal their thunder. Finally, you might establish a relationship with a friendly partnering prospect who would overwhelm an ambush—just be prepared to move quickly to close the deal if the ambush materializes, possibly through the use of some form of option contract that will allow you to do something if you need an option or alternative, such as when an ambush pops up.

Dr. Market's Observation:

 You might actually have a conversation with the ambusher about a confluence of interests. Maybe you should be working with each other rather than against. Be careful, but strange things can happen in the market.

Practical Experience—This Deserves a Maximum Weight of 3

Several years ago, when I was running Overseas Investment Missions, we delivered to the Chinese Rail Ministry a proposal to equip all passenger trains and railroad infrastructure with new GSM (the European cell phone technology) wireless equipment. Manufacture was to occur in China and passengers and the Rail Ministry would share much of the same equipment and services. No other bidders were evident during the last day of the bidding. You can imagine our surprise when we learned that Motorola had won the bid with a used old fashioned analog system they imported from the United States. Among the many lessons we took home was the knowledge that you can be ambushed by well-heeled competitors who remain out of sight until it is too late.

The possibility of ambush is one of many reasons you must build a powerful, focused, high-velocity launch. You must deflect the challenge. You can normally forecast the specific direction from which the ambush will come often by examining who or what is sitting 180° away from your field of view or expectation. Ordinarily, there should never be an ambush that is a surprise. I call this "McKnight's Rule of 180°." If there is going to be trouble, keep your eye on what is happening behind you. Conversely. if you are defeating a competitor, work your hardest 180° from his or her field of view.

Examples

Here are some excellent ambush situations where the action attracts attention and you have no control over who learns about it:

1. Announcing your revolutionary initiative before you have locked up the crucial resources.

2. Reselling telecommunications circuits to the U.S. government—insiders at the other carriers always have mischievous means by which to steal your traffic.

3. Manufacturing a coveted pharmaceutical product overseas.

4. Announcing a whopping operating margin in a business with meager barriers to entry.

The Coin-Operated Laundry— Ambush Exposure score: –5

It is not a healthy situation for you to be using equipment in the market where the manufacture could someday surprise you with a franchisee on attractive terms. You may survive for the first several years but if the franchise makes subsequent improvements and offers a steady stream of quality maintenance support you could find yourself ambushed. You could also find yourself ambushed by another firm that simply acquired the machines and installed them in competition with you. The score on this element is a negative. Ugly. While I am tempted to award it a –10, there are ways to get out of trouble and drive it toward a passing and therefore positive mark. I believe it deserves a –5.

Element 11, Ambush Exposure *score summary:*
Weight 3 x Score –5 = Total –15

Element 12

"HOT MARKET"

Tulip mania: A reckless mania for the purchase of tulip-bulbs in the seventeenth century. Beckmann says it rose to its greatest height in the years 1634–1637. A root of the species called Viceroy sold for £250; Semper Augustus, more than double that sum. The tulips were grown in Holland, but the mania which spread over Europe was a mere stock-jobbing speculation.
—E. Cobham Brewer, *Dictionary of Phrase and Fable*, 1898.

Definition

"Hot Markets" feature frantic buying, if not hoarding, of highly desired key products or services such as tickets to championship sporting events, responses to innovative terrorism, or defenses against epidemic. There is typically intense demand, limited time, and breathless enthusiasm for a solution. Buying habits may be irrational as hope trumps reality.

Relevance—Why Add This Element?

Unless you have a few million dollars to spare on your launch, you are likely to be positioning yourself to ask for money from others, particularly strangers. While "hot" markets are brief in duration, if your product satisfies a need that is quite intense, then irrational behavior can extend to the decisions made by customers and investors alike assisting you in launching your venture. If it is clear that wasting time will harm the prospects of a successful launch, then shortcuts will be taken and blemishes in the deal will become transparent.[1] Shortcuts can both help and hurt you, so be sure you understand the temperature of the market. You could be surprised how much of the deal can be recast in your favor without threatening the possibility of closing.

A "hot" market is the compelling, unserved need raised to an extraordinary and rarely seen level. The reason that we add an element for it is to help you understand when to pull out all the stops to launch instantly. This kind of market is an indicator of imminent and explosive growth.

Where to Find This Answer

The first step is to determine whether there is a widely recognized threat to a person or business. Then determine whether any prospective customer is intensely interested in acquiring a product or service to counter that threat. Now for the key question: Can your product solve the problem? Would anyone provide you with a

---

1. What is a "blemish?" Unless you are the Bill Gates of your industry, you could be a blemish. If you are new, uninformed, and lacking in sufficient funds of your own, you could be the biggest blemish of all. Other blemishes? Anything that would cause an investor to pause.

down payment in cash now on the mere hope that your product might work? Might there be other customers waiting for the same opportunity? This is the next level beyond Compelling Unserved Need. It is the element that measures crisis-solving, business/life saving, *critical* unserved need.

Score Elevation Tactics

It's not easy to manipulate a market to elevate its temperature in the 21st century. If there are no irrational buying habits and if there

---

Dr. Market's Caution:

 Assuming that the law is honored, if you are struggling with the ethics of convincing someone to buy your products when you do not believe they need them, what possesses you to believe that you know more than your customer about his or her needs? This sort of condescending behavior about market demand will almost certainly doom your ventures and if this is how you feel, you really should consider a career alternative to starting a business—or, for that matter, being in a business at all. On the other hand, duress and lying are all actionable, so don't go there either.

---

is no crisis looming for the customers, this item cannot score well. However, if it *does* score well, the odds are high that you could actually make a sale or two immediately. Few things are more impressive to vendors and investor prospects than approaches from entrepreneurs with customers in hand. Can you paint and validate a credible picture of imminent large-scale loss of opportunity or harm to existing assets or resources? Can you then portray your product as the perfect solution?

Practical Experience—This Deserves the Minimum Weight of 1

Computers, software, wireless voice and data, Y2K, fiber optic switching, the Internet, and deregulation of highly regulated monopolies have all enjoyed a time of spirited irrationality. The challenge is forecasting the next one—the best candidates could include antiterrorism solutions or solving a crisis in trustworthiness of corporate financial records.

Examples

Here are some possible ways to create or exploit new markets that could be "hot."

1. Watch for signs of an industry fad, then get into the game, and out of the game, during its steepest climb.

2. Watch for purchasing trends (the Web, chat rooms, and computer bulletin boards are excellent resources here), find an appropriate product (often available overseas at low cost because of lack of marketing savvy in the U.S.—they may not know enough about the U.S. to drive the price higher), and move quickly to fill as many orders as you can.

3. Aim your personal vision into the future about 4 to 6 years. Can you forecast any problems? Can you position your product today such that the problem will be inoculated by it? Can you prove it?

The Coin-Operated Laundry— "Hot Market" score: 2

While there is a nice technological advance working here with the ability to clean any stain into oblivion, there does not appear to be much warmth in the market. Given the potential for a trend in the market toward suits and dresses, the score should be positive but not by much. I would award it a 2. To elevate the score I would contact the suit manufacturers, the woolen manufacturers, and the creators and manufacturers of women's clothing. Use their sales forecasts to ascertain your demand. Will it be hot?

Element 12, "Hot Market" *score summary:*
Weight 1 x Score 2 = Total 2

PERSONAL

Introduction

Wise investors often look first on the personal side of a venture. The theory is that somehow demand, finance, process, and other matters can all be solved but if the people are not right, the odds of success become too remote to warrant further review. This section addresses the personal aspect of the venture as if it were the most important aspect to consider, despite the outcome of the questions relating to demand, capital, and other matters. The concern is justifiable. Few ventures flow smoothly from conception to harvest and the savvy investor knows that the enterprise will reach its objectives only with a smart, dedicated team that can convert threats into opportunities, and opportunities into value. A reminder is helpful: we are toying with questions that flow at the moment an idea is conceived, not when the idea has materialized in the market. This section is therefore something of a self-examination for you at a time when your idea is still cooped up in your imagination. Critically, "personal" is not intended for just one soul. It applies certainly to you and to all the other inside players as well. It relates to all the persons, most particularly to you.

Dr. Market's Warning:

 Get real! These next eight elements require you to be brutally frank about the toughest subject for you to view pragmatically—yourself. Try to be as realistic, candid, and practical as possible here.

Element 13

ATTITUDE OF CONFIDENCE AND FEARLESSNESS

The circulation of confidence is better than the circulation of money.
—James Madison, U S president. Speech at
Virginia Convention, June 20, 1788.

Definition

If ever there were any characteristics that would solve many shortcomings in a venture or new idea, it would be the attitude of confidence and fearlessness of the owner of the idea. Every other aspect of the venture can be solved by adding resources. However, if a positive attitude brimming with confidence and fearlessness is weak or missing, the chances are high that the venture will not succeed, at least with this person at the helm. Do you have what it takes to push your idea into reality? Are you positively glowing with confidence and fearlessness? Do you know how to swagger just a little bit?

Charles Swindoll, the famous theologian, described the value of attitude in his short essay on that subject. In the context of a new idea, the only attitude that is perfectly relevant seems to be that of confidence and fearlessness. Important nuances on the subject are visible in his essay:

> "The longer I live, the more I realize the impact of attitude on life. Attitude, to me, is more important than facts. It is more important than the past, than education, than money, than circumstances, than failures, than successes, than what other people think or say or do. It is more important than appearance, giftedness or skill. It will make or break a company ... a church ... a home. The remarkable thing is we have a choice every day regarding the attitude we will embrace for that day. We cannot change our past ... we cannot change the fact that people will act in a certain way. We cannot change the inevitable. The only thing we can do is play on the one string we have, and that is our attitude ... I am convinced that life is 10% what happens to me and 90% how I react to it. And so it is with you ... we are in charge of our Attitude."[1]

Confidence, the state of mind required to succeed, often brings with it a unique self-fulfilling power. It is almost as if, at the end of the day, when all things have been accounted for in the budget of actual contributions to the success story, there is a shortage, some missing element. Two and two equals only four when you needed five. The only thing that could account for the distance between the aggregated resources and success is something ephemeral, some intangible quality that attracts people and resources to a successful conclusion. That quality is a contagious attitude of confidence and fearlessness in the owner of the idea. You.

---

1. "Attitude" Charles Swindoll, *The Saturday Evening Post*, September-October, 1999.

Relevance—Why Add This Element?

The literature is quite modest about the role of attitude of confidence and fearlessness in launching a new venture. Some might view it as leadership. Some might view it as the natural extension of commitment. In the end however there is something almost supernatural about the element, possibly reflecting a gift that certain people have in bringing an idea into the market. Before this element can bloom, the person and/or the team must have substantial skills or knowledge in the field. They also require a certain gift of gab and the ability to weave a story quickly that grabs the attention of the listener. Do you have the right stuff?

Where to Find This Answer

Conversations with you, the owner of the idea, will offer insight into your level of confidence and fearlessness. Is there any justification for the confidence or fearlessness? Do you and/or your team come from the industry? Were you trained in the military to perform extraordinarily dangerous assaults (Marines, Rangers, Airborne, SEALs, and Special Forces are provided with training that gives them sufficient confidence to overwhelm armed opponents who are shooting at them—that is the quintessential confidence and fearlessness necessary to succeed)? Did you play confrontational contact sports? Were you on a school debate team? Were you ever close to the management of fiscal, market, or political power that won more than it lost? Do you have powerful friends in high places who will protect you? Is there some political wind blowing behind you or your idea? Do you tend to be an optimist and do you radiate that optimism to those around you?

Score Elevation Tactics

Elevating this score is rooted in your personal makeup, as was discussed above. If your personality or background do not deliver a sufficiently high score, find someone to manage the launch who does possess the correct attitude. Note that elevating the score does not necessarily mean manipulation. It means digging into your inner self to assure yourself that you have what it takes to succeed. Ask your spouse, your friends, those around you, and your children. It's too late to send yourself to charm school so you must elevate your score by digging into your self and your past. Do not be surprised if you have the right stuff. While teaching at the University of North Dakota, I was fortunate enough to teach the capstone course in management to three sections. In the course, we spent the first half on the substance of strategic planning and the second half on presentations from student teams. One team had a member named Bridgette Bata. She was extremely quiet yet very smart. When it came time for her to make her presentation, the class was simply astounded. She summoned up the most amazing confidence and fearlessness and we all applauded spontaneously after her 15 minutes had elapsed. The point? Somewhere deep inside, you could have just what Bridgette has. See if you can discover it now so that you can score well here.

Practical Experience—This Deserves a Weight of 2.

Confidence is one of the most significant personal attributes for the task ahead, and if you possess it, then mountains will move. Well, almost. My favorite image of confidence is Gertrude Bell, who made a seemingly impossible climb in the Alps and ended up having the mountain named after her.[2] When it comes to sports, the truly gifted players *believe* that they will succeed. It is not a suspicion or a hunch. The good ones actually believe it and it is that confidence that delivers the win, or at least one heck of an exciting contest.

Dr. Market's Observation:

When it comes to a new business idea, few things are more enchanting or contagious than watching a confident entrepreneur, brimming with fearlessness and energy, pursuing a dream. Can you behave this way?

Examples

Here are some people who possess an abundance of confidence and fearlessness:

1. Brett Favre, Doug Flutie, and the other NFL great quarterbacks.

2. Amelia Erhardt.

3. John Glenn and Neil Armstrong.

4. Ted Turner, my all-time favorite example for this element.

5. Gertrude Bell.

The Coin-Operated Laundry—Attitude of Confidence and Fearlessness score: 7

For this item you will need to insert your level of confidence and fearlessness. I am probably not a fair example—I tend to gleefully

---

2. Janet Wallach, *Desert Queen: The Extraordinary Life of Gertrude Bell: Adventurer, Advisor to Kings, Ally of Lawrence of Arabia.* Anchor Books, 1999.

tackle anything. Let's try a solid number that could use improvement, say, a 7. How do you improve this score? First I would build the opportunity so that the entrepreneur feels bullet-proof. This would entail improving the scores throughout this Innovator's Scorecard so that the aggregate score was high. This will impart a certain swagger that is unmistakable evidence of confidence and fearlessness. Second, I would make certain that the entrepreneur is financially safe and sound. Few things are more unnerving than trying to accomplish the impossible without knowing where your next mortgage payment will come from.

> Attitude of Confidence and Fearlessness *score summary:*
> Weight 2 x Score 7 = Total 14

Element 14

COMMITMENT

"There is one elementary truth, the ignorance of which kills countless ideas and splendid plans: the moment one definitely commits oneself, then providence moves too. All sorts of things occur to help one that never otherwise would have occurred. Whatever you can do, or dream you can do, begin it. Boldness has genius, power and magic in it. Begin it now."—Johann Wolfgang von Goethe
Faust, 1835, Translated from German

Definition

A commitment is an agreement or pledge to do something in the future, especially an engagement to assume a financial obligation at a future date or the state or an instance of being obligated or emotionally impelled. To be committed, the management must be prepared to devote their time, energy, and resources to this opportunity. Ideally, they would also contribute capital, something that should be part of most board of directors conversations. Furthermore, those on the board of directors must be prepared to devote a substantial portion of their days, be accessible every day,

109

and certainly acquire some of the equity with their own capital. Sometimes it really is all about commitment.

Relevance—Why Add This Element?

In the context of a new venture launch, the commitment of knowledgeable, well-connected managers and board members is often sufficient to fulfill Goethe's observation about its impact: There is truly "... genius, power and magic in it." On the other end of the spectrum, if there is no commitment, the key players are typically unavailable for critical decision making and leadership. They also deceive themselves into believing that they are committing enough if their name is on the list and if they provide some occasional chatter, say, once per month. Their time is simply too precious for them to be bothered. This is particularly true of people who routinely find themselves in the company of public figures—they cannot bother themselves with mundane matters such as launching new businesses. If they are committed to the idea, you have a chance to succeed. If they are not committed, you are wasting everyone's time. Personal commitment by the key players is therefore of considerable relevance as a predictor of success. It indicates that the team will be available for both the good times and the bad, something that investors, vendors, and charter customers will find consoling.

Where to Find This Answer

At this, the earliest stage of development, you can only state your case about your commitment and hope that the listeners buy in. However, if your day job is little short of miraculous, why should anyone believe that you are willing to commit 100% of your time to a fabulous new venture in Monaco? Your story needs to be compelling and convincing.

Score Elevation Tactics

If you need to bump this score higher, simply demonstrate maximum commitment. Your compensation and equity will be based upon full commitment from you, your management, and your board of directors. Other valuable souls who cannot commit can earn spots on the board of advisors. Most importantly, try to avoid creating unrealistic expectations that you and or all of your team will always be in harness, always pulling your weight. Investors will not believe that people holding bigger-than-life jobs are going to step down to commit to a startup. It is simply not realistic.

Dr. Market's Observation:

 One further observation—commitment is sometimes sought by investors who ask the entrepreneur to allow a lien on the family home. *Stop.* Do not go there, ever. The issue of commitment must be raised and resolved without anyone having to sign over the house. However, it could make sense to refinance your home into a low cost interest-only adjustable rate mortgage such as offered by RBC Mortgage Company, Lehman, or Chase Manhattan.

Practical Experience—This Element Deserves a Maximum Weight of 3

The Goethe quote is perhaps the most succinct statement of entrepreneurial truth I have ever seen expressed. It is often the source of the first sign of trouble in a great launch attempt. If the commitment is fractured, uneven, or simply missing in the team, you and the enterprise will have significant problems.

A low score is easy to calculate. Be realistic with yourself. A famous and accomplished surgeon, actually a wonderful soul, once tried to lead many people—including the royal family of the perfect host country—to believe that he would be the key medical mind behind a major new sports medicine facility to be located in the capital city. Money, talented surgeons, customers, land, host country, the Mediterranean Sea, and much more were organized and waiting. What more could you want? But the surgeon was unable to commit and it never came to pass. A great idea that would have significantly elevated the quality of sports health care in Europe was squandered by lack of commitment. In my experience, a lack of commitment by senior management is a compelling sign for you to depart the venture the instant it materializes.

Examples

Here are some examples of commitment helping overcome market intransigence.

1. Ted Turner and the notion of an ubiquitous news channel offered over cable television.

2. Motorola and its Iridium, an astounding success in commitment in the face of broad market apathy, never mind that there was little identifiable or quantifiable demand.

3. USA TODAY, which still seems to defy gravity, possibly because of its showcase editing, a Gannett uniqueness and hallmark.

The Coin-Operated Laundry—Commitment score: 6

Again, this is a personal item that will rely upon the personal circumstances of the entrepreneur and his or her immediate team. Let's give this another hypothetical score, a 6. Remember, you will be scoring this yourself so be realistic about how much time you can devote to this enterprise. The grading here should be tough. If the commitment is less than a 10, the enterprise could be in trouble. How do you improve the score? Insist upon exclusivity, either of yourself or of the person you are evaluating. Note that this is not the same as focus; it has everything to do with commitment toward success. You can be 150% committed and still drive a taxi cab to keep yourself alive until the funding arrives.

> Element 14, Commitment *score summary:*
> Weight 3 x Score 6 = Total 18

Element 15

STAYING POWER

Persistence can grind an iron beam down into a needle.
—Chinese proverb

Nothing in the world can take the place of Persistence. Talent will not; nothing is more common than unsuccessful men with talent. Genius will not; unrewarded genius is almost a proverb. Education will not; the world is full of educated derelicts. Persistence and Determination alone are omnipotent. The slogan "Press On" has solved and will always solve the problems of the human race.
—Calvin Coolidge, U S president. Broadside distributed to agents of the New York Life Insurance Company, 1932. Former President Coolidge was at the time a director of the New York Life Insurance Company.

Definition

Staying power solves the question of what happens if you run out of cash. It entails persistence, the ability to generate consulting or other out-of-pocket income, personal savings, support from a doting relative, and so on. It depends upon cost of living, family circumstances, a working spouse, stamina, and the general wherewithal to carry on if there is no cash.

Relevance—Why Add This Element?

Few ventures are funded quickly enough to carry a cash-poor entrepreneur. To succeed, you may need to develop and sustain a separate source of income. This will derive financial stamina and the ability to persist as the funding process takes its time to bloom. One reason why repeat entrepreneurs are so valuable to the economy is this element of staying power—they can simply outwait the funding process.

Staying Power gauges whether you will be able to arrive at the finish line during the funding process. If not, then you will vanish and few will think to send you a thank you.

Dr. Market's Observation:

 Note the possibility that the investors will, if they sense limited resources, be tempted to delay closing until they can accumulate a significantly greater portion of the equity (if you don't think this is possible or true, you need to abandon the entrepreneurial track and find a job somewhere—it's a tough game and people play rough). The solution? Create staying power for yourself and your team.

Where to Find This Answer

Staying power is often observed best by simple inquiry. How do you expect to live while the funding becomes organized? What will your references say and what will the results of investigations uncover in any entrepreneurial disasters in which you played a part—did you hang tough or did you cut and run? So, be honest with yourself here.

Score Elevation Tactics

The easiest way to elevate this score is to make certain you can create adequate consulting or other hourly work to carry yourself through lean times if they are encountered. With good fortune, your work will be in a field that is complementary to the enterprise, perhaps somewhere in the value chain. Of course, the best source of cash is to pre-sell products or services before you write the business plan or raise the first big round of funding—it's easier than you think.

Practical Experience—This Deserves the Medium Weight of 2

There are few tactics more valuable in starting a new business than adding a period to the game if you are losing. While that is fantasy in sports, it is a rational strategy for strong ideas and compelling opportunities if you cannot reach your launch objective in a reasonable time. You simply outwait market opposition. How many ventures fail because they exhaust their resources only to watch a look-alike take the idea and bloom in the marketplace? If the investor and other resource vendors can be assured of your staying power, a successful launch is far more certain to occur. Entrepreneurs with financial resources, light-burden second jobs, or a financially robust spouse are often critical to successful ventures. It is certainly true that more than 50% of the launches that were successful in my classrooms over the last seven years succeeded because the entrepreneur was able to carry him or herself during the lean times just before substantial funding arrived.

Examples

Here are some ways people have lived two lives while their business grew.

1. Consultant who worked for her clients in the morning and saved all her afternoons for her new company.

2. The college dropouts who built their own computer and operating system in the garage while living at home (think Apple).

3. A hobby enterprise you run while carrying a full-time job elsewhere.

4. A spouse who can keep the roof over your head while you invade the new market.

The Coin-Operated Laundry—Staying Power score: 6

Can you (including your insider team) hang tough without pay until after the funding arrives? How long can you last? What is the nature of your support—will your support threaten the enterprise in any way with added time? Let's pretend the score is a 6. How can it be improved? Look for consulting work for the team or the individuals on the team. Look for work for their spouses! Rent their barn. Use space they own for special warehousing needs. Just make certain that precious resources are covered.

Element 15, Staying Power *score summary:*
Weight 2 x Score 6 = Total 12

Element 16

PASSION

There are only two powers in the world—the spirit and the sword; and in the long run the sword will always be conquered by the spirit.
—Napoleon Bonaparte

Definition

Passion is a potent elixir that works well in small doses and is toxic in abundance. Using *Merriam-Webster*, here are the relevant definitions: *Passion, fervor, ardor, enthusiasm*, and *zeal* mean intense emotion compelling action. *Passion* applies to an emotion that is deeply stirring or ungovernable <was a slave to his *passions*>. *Fervor* implies a warm and steady emotion <read the poem aloud with great *fervor*>. *Ardor* suggests warm and excited feeling likely to be fitful or short-lived <the *ardor* of their honeymoon soon faded>. *Enthusiasm* applies to lively or eager interest in or admiration for a proposal, cause, or

119

activity <never showed much *enthusiasm* for sports>. *Zeal* implies energetic and unflagging pursuit of an aim or devotion to a cause <preaches with fanatical *zeal*>. But, note the dark undercurrent— "ungovernable," "short-lived," and "fanatical."

Relevance—Why Add This Element?

Passion is a key aspect of the leadership and confidence required to be the entrepreneur who successfully converts and inspires people to the cause. It is relevant to the successful startup because it serves as an intellectual and emotional energizer that ignites listeners and supporters so that the enterprise plunges forward. Passion often carries the entrepreneur through the antagonism, doubt, criticism, apathy, and ennui that often occur in the marketplace. Without passion you will fail to have that extra edge required to put the ball over the goal line.

Where to Find This Answer

Passion is most accurately measured by the way you conduct yourself as you tell the story. How enthusiastic do you become? Do you spill out the details of your enterprise spontaneously? Can you recover instantly from a tough question about demand or product features that, frankly, had never crossed your mind before? Do you constantly tumble your product, your customers, and your prospective venture over and over in your mind? Does it occupy your every waking thought? Do you find yourself anticipating the key questions and rehearsing an eye-popping response? Do you find that you come up with uncannily brilliant thinking when backed into a corner by a prospective investor or vendor?

Score Elevation Tactics

Coaching is often the solution here, either to raise a low score or to diminish passion that is actually harmful to the prospects of winning the funding or other resource or customer you are approaching. Attempting to drive a launch without passion is not only difficult, it is almost impossible. On the other hand, "getting carried away" is also counter productive and must be avoided. Search for the middle ground.

Practical Experience—This Deserves the Minimum Weight of 1

Passion is one of the drivers of a launch. Without it, there will probably be no future. It can come in a variety of doses. Some entrepreneurs run hot. Some run really cool. But the critical essence of passion is the capacity to attack your challenges with the glee, acumen, and aplomb of someone who simply cannot be denied. Real winners get into a "zone" and are almost extraterrestrial in their capacity to anticipate and lead the team to a win.

Dr. Market's Observation:

 It is uncanny how difficult it is to predict whether a person will have the requisite passion to succeed until after they take the leadership reins and say "giddyup." At this early moment in your idea's existence, you need to dive in as if your life depended on your success.

Examples

Observe the passion with which the following companies were developed and grown from scratch: Microsoft, Southwest Air, Sun Microsystems, Intel, McCaw, Cisco, eBay, Amazon.com, EMS, Apple, Cisco, and many more. The leadership was brimming with passion, which delivered the energy for the launch.

The Coin-Operated Laundry—
Passion score: 7

Not too much now, remember that this is a delicate elixir. Some is required, and too much might be toxic. Let's pretend you have a 7. How do you improve the score? Learn more of the details about the business—listeners normally mistake mastery of details for passion. This goes for your vendors, your products, your capabilities, your benefits, and your customer base. Passion in the context of the Coin-Operated Laundry is to load the typical work schedule with sufficient customers to account for all of your costs and then some. All the other revenues would simply represent the margin.

> Element 16, Passion *score summary:*
> Weight 1 x Score 7 = Total 7

Element 17

MANAGEMENT COMPETENCE

Skill and confidence are an unconquered army.
—George Herbert

Definition

Conventional wisdom says that the person who spawns the idea could struggle in actually managing the launch. The key to assessing management competence is the ability of you, the idea person, to realistically acknowledge your shortcomings and assess your management skills. Are you up to the tasks? This element is also slightly premature in these very earliest moments of the idea's existence. How can anyone tell *what* your competence will be? But it is a useful reminder of how important management competence will become when capital is discussed with prospective investors. Can your

123

team reach its objectives in a timely fashion? How confident are you
with being at the helm? If you acknowledge your shortcomings now,
when is it that you expect to "get out of the way?" Or can you
repackage and retrain yourself so that you are up to the job in the
longer term?

Relevance—Why Add This Element?

After the idea has captured their imagination, competent
management is the highest priority of sophisticated investors.
This principle of sound venture launching is premised upon the
fact that in good times or bad, competent management will
exploit all opportunities and convert all threats into blessings.
Investors bet on people who can manage well in all
circumstances. It reduces the risk that the invested funds will be
lost, and that they will be lodged in a priority position in a
successful harvest.

Where to Find This Answer

It is not hard to see a winner in a new entrepreneur. Common
traits include relevant skills and experience in the industry,
confidence, commitment, fearlessness, realism, honesty, attentive
listening, and so on. What is your realistic assessment of how you
will perform? Can you lead a team of complementary yet diversely
skilled winners to a successful launch and harvest? Will the
inevitable due diligence by the investors either now or later
uncover some flaw in your makeup that threatens your ability to
lead effectively?

Score Elevation Tactics

The easiest way to solve a soft score here is to simply accomplish what the doubters believe you cannot do. Make some sales to customers. Prevail upon a collection of solid winners in their fields to join you on the executive team. Form a first-class set of boards, both directors and advisors. If you can accomplish these things immediately, who can legitimately doubt your capabilities to lead the enterprise through its launch and growth? Until you make a mistake, no one will have an excuse to criticize you. The problem

Dr. Market's Observation:

Once a solid executive team core has been established, say a CEO and a COO and a marketer with perhaps a board member or two, stop looking for help. Trust that the core team, if exemplary, will be able to attract the appropriate additions to solidify your success. Note that the CFO position should consist of nothing more than a bookkeeper at first. You will need a full-time CFO when you start actually paying income taxes because it is at that point that you will have financial dynamics in play that go beyond accounting. More often than not, the decision to hire a CFO will be made when you receive money from a sophisticated investor—they often have a CFO candidate in mind. Instead, try to use a small accounting firm for your bookkeeping matters and plug in a rational "salary" for their services. They are less likely to get involved in some political maneuvering to undermine the investor's confidence in your capabilities. At this tender stage in taking your idea to market, you need stability and accounting accuracy, not politics.

at this early moment in the life of the company is that you may not have the time to demonstrate your prowess.

Practical Experience—This Deserves the Maximum Weight of 3

Management competence varies widely depending upon the experience of the CEO. Strong CEOs pick reliable, well-qualified people whom they can trust to accomplish the company's objectives. Weak CEOs often overemphasize loyalty and try to slot their pals into jobs that they are ill-suited to fill. A frequent error here is to choose the quiet, taciturn intellect, a close friend of the CEO, who has long fancied himself or herself to be a superb marketer. Try *not* to allocate jobs or expectations of jobs to anyone at this early stage. At most you should "pencil" people into key slots and retain your ability to move people around. This is the last time you will have that flexibility.

In the "virtual" corporation a team's expertise is cobbled together irrespective of the members' locations. A virtual group can handle the early stages of planning the enterprise, but once production is set to begin, you need a central location and most of your team needs to be there. Yet virtual enterprises are a permanent fixture of the entrepreneurial landscape. If you have off-site members of your management team, the most important question is whether they are committed to the enterprise. The trap of course is that too many top-drawer executives hedge their bets with multiple commitments, a self-inflicted divide-and-conquer policy that could doom your venture.

Dr. Market's Observation:

If you are the person with the idea, do not be too quick to abandon your post as CEO. If you can attract advisors around you there will be little substitute for the passion, commitment, staying power, confidence, and fearlessness you can bring to bear. This is particularly true if you can attract revenues now, up front. There is no reason why you *must* step down if you demonstrate that you can create and run your business from day one.

Examples

There are many examples of entrepreneurs who stayed the course into their company's growth and maturity. Bill Gates, Ted Turner, Charley Ergen (EchoStar), and Larry Ellison are all trophy winners who didn't have many clues about what they were doing on the day before day one.

The Coin-Operated Laundry— Management Competence score: 4

According to our assumptions for this hypothetical example, you are alone and your idea requires a team. Let's assume you know the business. You are still not competent to cover all the bases simultaneously. The score at this moment in the enterprise's existence is a 4—this is a flunking score that you must strive to elevate to at least a 7 or 8. How can it be improved? Add beef. Whatever your skills, remove them from the mix of requirements and find a couple of people who can cover the difference. This one is easy to fix. Be careful to add people who are genuinely qualified to manage their positions—no pals inserted into positions for which they fancy themselves to be perfectly suited.

Element 17, Management Competence *score summary:*
Weight 3 x Score 4 = Total 12

Element 18

HONESTY AND
INTEGRITY

*I am sure that in estimating every man's value either in private or
public life, a pure integrity is the quality we take first into
calculation, and that learning and talents are only the second.*
—Thomas Jefferson, U S president. Letter, June 15, 1792, to
John Garland Jefferson. *The Papers of Thomas Jefferson*,
vol. 24, p. 82, ed. Julian P. Boyd, et al., 1950.

Definition

Do the individuals in the company enjoy a reputation for high
honesty and integrity? High honesty and integrity for an
entrepreneur could mean something different from what it means to
a seasoned veteran senior vice president at General Motors. The
entrepreneur may have a much simpler view of integrity and honesty
rooted in the Golden Rule. The person from GM will view honesty
and integrity with a more complicated and sophisticated perspective
that is guided by the laws swirling around a publicly traded
company and the company's policies and culture. Taking into

129

consideration the alarm bells set off by Enron, at least the entrepreneur has the Golden Rule to rely upon.

Relevance—Why Add This Item?

Sadly, the Enron/Tyco/WorldCom/Global Crossing/Adelphia disasters are responsible for the closest we may have come so far to a complete breakdown in confidence in our accounting/financial reporting systems. As the senior executives of these disgraced companies (and in particular the accounting profession!) have now discovered, honesty and integrity will not go out of style for long in corporate America. Too much is riding on it. Honesty and integrity are particularly important in situations such as yours, where it is an indelible penalty in the eyes of seed investors if you or any member of your team suffer from an image problem in these areas.

Dr. Market's Observation:

 Special circumstances surround entrepreneurs who are ex-convicts. Different rules must apply. They have served their social debt and they are launching a venture that offers employment and possibly riches. The trick is attracting the capital and other resources required for a safe launch. One consideration is the ability to launch an enterprise in such a way as to derive early cash flows and move the later investor's gaze past the early times, when honesty and integrity would be under heavier scrutiny. In other words, for some people honesty and integrity just might be an "earn-out" over time. We don't have to look far to uncover bad behavior in society today (it is too often on display in professional sports).

Where to Find This Answer

References are the traditional means to prove your honesty and integrity. What will your references say? Perhaps more importantly, what will industry insiders say about you? What will the newspaper archives and the clerks' offices of the various jurisdictions in which you have lived say? Perhaps the best way for investors to learn about these issues is to find people who once worked for or around you. They will seek out old enemies and see whether they can be lured into impugning your honesty and integrity. You can hope your enemies will acknowledge that the old conflict was attributable entirely to interpersonal chemistry. However, since the Scorecard is designed for an up-front snapshot, this element is not an easy fit—it takes time to discover the answers. Grade yourself by anticipating the answers, and make sure your résumé is accurate.

Dr. Market's Observation:

 If you are suddenly unemployed and you have never worked in the industry you are pursuing, you have a number of issues regarding your lack of experience. Honesty and integrity are likely *not* to be among those issues. You will probably have a clean slate here, so insert the high number you may deserve and move on. If you truly deserve a low number because of your past, insert the low number and return to this element for remediation and score elevation later.

Score Elevation Tactics

Burnishing a poor reputation could require the use of a public relations agent or an attorney, either of whom could track down rumors, collect important data, and pour salve onto raw feelings. Within limits, a poor reputation can be overcome and this score can be significantly increased. The key is to distract the investor with the value and corporate goodwill that has been created. One important question will be, is it worth it?

Practical Experience—This Deserves the Maximum Weight of 3

This element can be tricky. Behavior that trampled on my sense of honor and integrity long ago is now trivial and unworthy of concern. However, given the experience we are having with WorldCom, Enron, Tyco, and others, a lack of integrity can no longer be taken lightly. The key is learning about your own reputation up front.

Is a convicted felon incapable of building a reputation of honesty and integrity? Before you leap to answer, note that there are some genuinely first-class individuals out there who are ex-convicts.[1] Perhaps the smartest thing is to avoid generalizations and instead dwell on the specifics of an individual's background. Have there been allegations of wrongdoing involving SEC rules or generally accepted accounting principles? If so, you should consider wrapping yourself in the protective cocoon of a fine team and removing yourself from being named as an officer or board member of the company.

---

1. As a matter of practice I typically do not avoid working with ex-convicts who are attempting to launch new businesses. Yes, I need to know them, but these days it is just not hard at all to know someone who has served time in prison. Besides, it is always interesting to see how people carry the bricks that life gives them to carry.

> ## Dr. Market's Observation:
>
> Entrepreneurs don't hold jobs. They create jobs and opportunity and wealth. Sometimes that means that they are expected to do things that are not fun, like missing payments on their bills. Poor FICO credit scores are not where you look for honesty and integrity problems on entrepreneurs. The biggest thieves in corporate America pay their bills on time.

Examples

People with special issues in the area of honesty and integrity include Mike Milken, Mike Deaver, Bill Clinton, Marv Albert, Ollie North, Pete Rose, and Jerry Springer. All seem to have survived their bouts with notoriety and all seem fully capable of showing up in a dazzling success story in a newspaper article near you. Fences can be mended.

The Coin-Operated Laundry—Honesty and Integrity score: 8

For the sake of our model, we are assuming that you have good honesty and integrity. Let's say you have assigned yourself an 8. How can it be improved? First of all, where are the dents? How nasty are the foibles? Isolate them and address them one by one. Get to your biggest antagonists and neutralize them with honey or countervailing arguments. Sometimes a little old-fashioned saber rattling never hurt anyone—defamation of character is something that might be actionable, so if someone threatens you with it, give some thought to seeking legal counsel. Make certain however that none of your admirers get carried away. As an old pal named Rene Anselmo used to say, "don't ever waste a minute on revenge. Let God do that for you." Just go about cleaning up your mess and hope that no one looks too hard.

Element 18, Honesty and Integrity *score summary:*
Weight 3 x Score 8 = Total 24

Element 19

SUCCESS ETHIC

The toughest thing about success is that you've got to keep on being a success. Talent is only a starting point in business. You've got to keep working that talent.
—Irving Berlin

Definition

Winners are magnetic. They have a knack for leadership and their records list noteworthy successes. They know how and when to inspire people to make sacrifices (within reason) for the good of the team and the achievement of the goal. They have experienced a championship surge that has at least put them in contention for the gold medal, the league championship, or the respect and adoration of their peers.

Dr. Market's Observation:

Note that a reputation for having a strong success ethic should not be used as camouflage for cutting corners; this behavior can result in conduct that will flunk due diligence when the next round of funding occurs. Angela Dows of the University of North Dakota once observed that when it was all said and done, it was the culture of success-at-all-costs that doomed Enron more than anything else and when it was time for them to merge with another company, the due diligence caused the deal to collapse. Amen.

Relevance—Why Add This Element?

All investors hate to lose their money. One of their techniques for protecting their investment is to migrate toward deals managed by people who know how to win. Sometimes these people say things that could trouble the legal advisor. Sometimes they coerce or cajole in ways that would never look good in writing, including political incorrectness. These people win and they are prepared to do what is necessary to deliver. A separate book can be written on the number of great companies that began their existence doing something quite different from what they do today. The reason is the persistent drive for success by a management team that was not as enamored with the means as they were with their obligation to succeed. After all, the business launch game is about converting a small amount of money into a large amount of money as quickly as possible. Nothing is possible without success, and success is not possible without people driving the enterprise who know success and how to reach it. These are the champions who know how to manipulate the clock, the resources, the playing field, and the play of the game so that success is achieved more times than not. They remember the joy of a championship win and they understand that the rewards cascade over their heads like a piñata bursting with prizes. That is why this element must be added to the mix—it's critical to success.

Where to Find This Answer

What have you done in the past that would indicate that you are capable of achieving a significant win? Can you work in a situation filled with enigma and ambiguity? Are you a self-guided missile? Are you capable of identifying and running through false stop signs? Can you withstand a staggering hit as if nothing had happened? Can you add a new fifth quarter to the game? Can you maneuver your resources down the field outside the "out of bounds" marker? What in your record or the record of your teammates suggests that you have this "right stuff?"

Dr. Market's Observation:

Having a success ethic does not mean that you must have an unblemished record. Some professional investors are troubled when there are no missteps, no failures. They wonder, will this be your first? The key is being familiar with the taste of winning, not having a record that has no failures (such a record might flunk the investor's snicker test).

Score Elevation Tactics

Elevating this score is an exercise in attracting people to your team who are seasoned in and understand the dynamics of success. You will need to convince your investors that you are prepared to listen to and work with your team. You must build the confidence of the investor that you and your people can win this game.

Practical Experience—This Deserves the Medium Weight of 2

Winners know how to push, scrap, argue vigorously, and elbow their way into the goal. They also know when to cooperate, be silent, be patient, and cover their position no matter how unpleasant it is, without complaint. Most remarkably they know when to turn up their energy, creativity, and skill simultaneously with the others on the team. They have a capacity to reach unheard-of heights of accomplishment, something I call a "championship surge." It is an awesome characteristic and one that I seek in every team. One of my all-time favorites is Mr. Blaise Larson of the University of North Dakota. Blaise named his team's enterprise "The Code" and crafted a remarkably well-reasoned financial section of the business plan for his team's company, which is setting the global standard for DNA portraiture. The business plan won the North Dakota State Championship for business plans on January 15, 2003. Blaise also happened to be the starting fullback for the Fighting Sioux football team, NCAA Champions 2001, Division II. Winning the state championship on the business plan is also solid evidence of the success ethic of the CEO, Ms. Erin Dolezal.

Examples

There are plenty of winners out there who know and understand the championship surge. Here are some who are particularly praiseworthy:

1. Tiger Woods.

2. Mia Hamm.

3. Kerri Strug (Remember her? She won the Olympic gold in gymnastics with a broken foot. Awesome!).

4. Roger Staubach.

5. The entire women's Olympic hockey teams from both the United States and Canada during the last two winter Olympics.[1]

6. Jack Nicklaus.

The Coin-Operated Laundry—Success Ethic score: 6

What can you say about your experience at conquering something, anything that is impossible? Have you ever been involved in a championship game? Have you ever won a contest in music? Theater? Or any other confrontation with an opponent that involved your intellect and your personal performance? These are cues of your success ethic and for this case let's assume you score a 6. How can it be improved? The first order of business is to not

---

1. Three of the participants in these two astounding gold medal finals, Katie King (USA), Beckie Kellar (Canada), and Tera Mounsie (USA), also played on the 1997 Ivy League Champion softball team from Brown University, along with a fleet-footed center fielder named Katie McKnight, the author's daughter. All of these wonderful athletes have experienced the championship surge.

fake it. No trumped-up facts. The reason is that it will catch up with you when you stand to lose the most. So, the best way to overcome shortcomings here is to find someone or a couple of people for the leadership of your management team who know how to win. Most importantly, listen and watch how they go about winning your championship for you.

Element 19, Success Ethic *score summary:*
Weight 2 x Score 6 = Total 12

Element 20

LOOKING GOOD
IN THE LOBBY

My son has said to me that if you want to participate actively with businessmen today, keep your hair cut, stand straight and don't talk about the past.
—Cyrus Eaton (at age 84)

Definition

Looking Good in the Lobby is an element that comes to us from Steve Halstedt of Centennial Ventures in Denver, one of the lions of the venture capital industry. It addresses your professional and social acceptability. Are you presentable to a group of investors? Can you carry the conversation during the "dog and pony" shows? Can the investor envision inviting you to stay overnight at the house and meeting the family? Would the investor mind being stuck on the same island with you for a couple of years (because in an odd sort of way, that is exactly what's about to happen)?

141

This extends to the presentation itself, and the ease with which you are able to tell the story. Specifics include weight, dress, personal hygiene, fragrance, manner of speech, hair, teeth, jewelry, and your ability to reiterate the story from the heart while looking them in the eye, especially with an effective PowerPoint presentation.

Dr. Market's Observation:

 The looking-good element also applies to your conversations with vendors, prospective customers, and the management team you hope to attract. These conversations will hopefully occur prior to your publication of the business plan.

Relevance—Why Add This Element?

Starting a new venture is no picnic. If you are someone out of the zone of acceptability, the investor often has plenty of opportunities to work with people who do indeed "look good in the lobby." If life is too short to be miserable, why work with a slob? Now before you bury a great idea because you don't dress like a collegian, stop. You need to remember that this element simply means you must conform to a zone of acceptability. If you have developed a strain of buckwheat that conquers cancer, you are allowed to look like a farmer or a biophysicist. No problem. But if you expect to maneuver the business through the traps of the investment game, you will need to look like, act like, and work like a winning entrepreneur. This element could be considerably more important than you will want it to be. It is here because it deserves to be honored in launching a new business.

Where to Find This Answer

Your appearance and manner are perhaps the first things you convey to a listener, and the first impression is a lasting one. Frankly, you will know in the first five minutes of your conversation with an investor how you are being perceived.[1] Do you look the part? And for what part are you the perfect candidate? CEO or Sr. VP Development, with a seat on the board of directors and a large portion of founder's stock? Clues are certain to come your way; read them.

Score Elevation Tactics

If your score here is less than 9, put yourself through a quick charm school. Openly acknowledge what needs to be done and address the matter up front and quickly. If there is a problem and you are unable to make the necessary adjustments, then the score must remain low. In the end however, remember that this is only one of many elements to be scored in the first few moments of a venture or idea's existence. There are many stories of people in elevated positions in corporate America who arrived on the scene in fairly

---

1. How can you get your cues beforehand? Two pieces of commonly available equipment could do wonders for you. Borrow or purchase a small dictation recorder and practice your pitch as if speaking over the phone. Next, borrow or purchase a small video camera and record your pitch. Then look at yourself on the monitor. Practice, practice, practice. As for personal grooming and style of dress, circumstances play a role. Can you do well without combing your hair and while being a bit gamy? Sure, but only if you have been on a week-long sail with your investor candidate. A good rule? Keep yourself scrubbed up, no bad smells, neat hair, and a style of clothing "one notch above" (e.g., if they are in a sports shirt or blouse, you are in a blazer. If they are in a blazer and no tie or a skirt and blouse, you wear a tie or a dress. Normally you don't have to wear the tux or gown if they are in a business suit). And *never* go in with bad shoes. Welcome to the world of sales.

rough condition. The point? A low score here can be cured quickly with diligence and energetic attention to the details of "looking good in the lobby." Start working on it now and don't show up at the dance with a score below 9.

Practical Experience—This Deserves the Minimum Weight of 1

Appearances do indeed influence decision makers. Suits, ties, white shirts, shined shoes, businesslike yet attractive dresses, a simple strand of pearls, and the quality of the PowerPoint presentation all speak volumes about the image that you hope to convey. Can your behavior exude credibility and self-confidence? Are you an extrovert (good) or introvert (not so good)? Are you upbeat, happy, convivial, and a joy to be around? Or are you moody, morose, secretive, and constantly referring to matters that are solved only through your unidentified "friends?" Perhaps most importantly, do you know the substance of the business?

You should be used in the presentations unless there is a problem. If there *is* a problem, do not be unreasonable, just expect to be placed into a plausible yet highly respected position and let the team move on toward everyone's objectives. There is no substitute for success.

Examples

My favorite example of this element occurred when I sat down for breakfast with the founder and CEO of EchoStar, years ago. Charley was already a huge success and he had just visited the orthodontist. His teeth were wrapped in metal, and he was improving his score on "looking good in the lobby."

The Coin-Operated Laundry—Looking Good in the Lobby score: 6

This has a lot to do with personal appearance, style, poise, personality, taste, grace, ability to work with strangers, and a long list of other "soft" characteristics that we all learn have more to do with success than we ever imagined. Let's assume we have a slightly low score here, a 6, so that we can go about improving ourselves. The best way is to go through a quick crash course. Put yourself in the hands of your spouse and her or his pals. Stop by the local haberdasher/dress shop. Bleach the teeth. Work out in the gym. Manicure the nails (you too guys!). Lose 10 pounds, 20 if you can. Memorize the PowerPoint presentation to the point where you actually know what it is trying to say, and then forget the notes. When you stand and give your presentation, deliver it from the heart, looking them square in the eyes, and move around a little to impart a *slight* sense of power, passion, and urgency.

> Element 20, Looking Good in the Lobby *score summary:*
> Weight 1 x Score 6 = Total 6

OPERATIONS

Introduction

This section consists primarily of those elements that address your ability to reach your objectives in a timely fashion. As Steve Bannon at Jeffries Bannon Media Group once explained, "When you launch a newbie you need to have enough muzzle velocity to place your payload somewhere over the moon, because the moon is often just about how far your objective will appear to be." The elements in this section involve speed, weight, trajectory, and many other matters that you will need to groom and provision your idea and venture for the long ride to your objectives.

Element 21

CASH FLOWING NOW

Better eight hundred in cash than a thousand on credit.
—Chinese proverb.

Definition

Cash flow is self-explanatory. Can you receive revenues now? The definition of "now" can be flexible—now could mean up to 90 days or so. But the point stands. If you can derive revenues very soon, even partial revenues as earnest money deposits, then this element scores highly. Can you attract revenues prior to the publication of the business plan?

Relevance—Why Add This Element?

It is nearly always possible to attract revenue early. The cash does not need to exceed your costs—it only needs to be generated in pursuit of the enterprise's mission. It moves the wheels of progress. Suddenly marketing, operations, finance, human resources, and the legal machinery all function together to build the company's business and culture.

Where to Find This Answer

How do you know whether you can attract cash? Find a willing and qualified listener and ask for the order. If they cannot justify a large purchase, ask for a small one or a charter customer discount. If you cannot deliver immediately, ask for an advance. If the buyer could become an enormous customer, attach a warrant for stock. If they can place an enormous order as the number *two* customer, attach two warrants (an attempt to ward off the one-trick-pony syndrome where you could wake up someday with no business and a new owner, the only customer who stepped up when you launched your business). To be sure, this is the first moment of the venture's existence and the odds may be high that you will not begin the conversations with a check in hand from a panting customer. Can you *forecast* the early movement of cash? Better yet, can you reach out and make a quick sale or two? Now?

Score Elevation Tactics

It should be possible, even in the worst circumstances, to ship some product or service to a customer or two now. The key could be to borrow the plant and other fixed assets necessary to move it. Certainly, some value-added resource or service could be helpful. However it should not be impossible to serve a couple of your customers now. A letter of credit for a large number of your products, conditioned upon the fact that they exist and pass certain minimum standards of quality, can be a great way to generate early cash. Ask yourself whether this will be possible and score the element accordingly.

Dr. Market's Observation:

 Make sure you have sewn up protection from your vendors who might otherwise exploit your success by creating a new competitor. Your lawyer can help you after you achieve a passing score on the Scorecard.

Practical Experience—This Deserves the Medium Weight of 2

The teams that were able to attract cash from a customer before they had written a business plan nearly always succeeded. Orders built confidence and signaled all the supporters and resource vendors that this was a real opportunity. There is a troublesome question waiting for the team that cannot attract a customer now: What makes you think that anyone will buy your product or service later? It is possible that you do not have a business, unless you convince a prospective customer to part with some cash (or an irreversible commitment to pay cash) now.

Examples

The revenues can come from any relevant endeavor. Wood distribution can precede a furniture manufacturing business. Collecting used tires can precede a distributorship in the sale of new tires. Buying telecommunications capacity in bulk can precede the sale of small chunks of time on circuits that generate immediate revenues on a competitor's satellites while you design, procure, build, and launch your own. Naturally the optimum solution to this element is to actually sell products or services that will come from your team. There is nearly always something you can do to begin the business immediately.

The Coin-Operated Laundry—Cash Flowing Now score: 7

In our hypothetical case, we have a new business. The question then is, would it be possible to attract cash within, say, 30 to 60 days? This would be possible because of the use of other people's resources, including possibly our competition.[1] This type of

---

1. This is the sign of a smart player in the business *but* you need to be careful. How would I help a competitor? I would consider offering overflow, backup capacity for their operation. Then *they* would need to be careful because my students all know what to do with a real customer. You would probably be positioning your business in the wholesale end of the spectrum. If you gain traction here, guess what just happened? Your business morphed a little bit into the path of a greater success potential. To use a baseball/softball metaphor, you just positioned your hit ball into a trajectory that will bring it to earth in fair territory without being caught by a competitor. It may only be a single, but it's still a hit.

business should be worthy of a 7 to start. Increasing that score could mean landing some long-term, high-volume contracts with an aggressive driver pickup and delivery program. Once your plant was operational, you would simply start using your equipment the next day. You should be able to be in business within 30 to 60 days.

Element 21, Cash Flowing Now *score summary:*
Weight 2 x Score 7 = Total 14

Element 22

REVENUE MODEL THAT SWAMPS COSTS

It is a socialist idea that making profits is a vice.
I consider the real vice is making losses.
—Winston Churchill

Definition

Now we come to the classic though highly abbreviated definition of a going enterprise. Can you foresee that revenues will swamp the costs, all the costs, such that you can earn an adequate return for the investors? Possible costs include manufactured unit purchase, consulting, service fees, use fees, lease, value pricing, commission upon sale or closing, and so on. To what extent can you foresee that you will be able to cover all your costs, fixed and marginal? Quick, right now, can you say that there is a business here?

Relevance—Why Add This Element?

Too often this element is ignored in new business launching.
Starting and running a business is not a giveaway. This element has
to be added to ensure that you are not trying to run a church or a
charitable organization. While you have only just begun the
analysis of the enterprise that you might build behind your idea,
the sooner it is evident that a going enterprise can be built around
it, the sooner you will be able to embark upon your journey. Until
this element scores well, your idea will be idle with no place to go.
It is almost embarrassing to add this element to the mix, but too
often it kicks up a surprise that needs to be resolved prior to
moving forward.

Where to Find This Answer

Assessing whether revenues will swamp costs is among the most
intuitive of the Scorecard tasks you will undertake just now. With
added experts brought into the dialog, this score will become more
reliable. You need to be familiar with the cost side of the business.
What will it take to deliver your products or services to market?
What is your expected selling price? How many units do you
expect to sell and when will you receive the revenues?

Score Elevation Tactics

It may be possible to pursue more than one revenue model.
Newspapers attract revenues with advertising and revenues from
copy sales through subscription and newstands. IBM attracts

revenues for both manufactured units sold and consulting. What are your primary means (plural) of revenue generation? On the cost side, can you foresee how you can drive your costs down?

Practical Experience—This Deserves the Minimum Weight of 1

A surprising number of times, the model cannot cover the costs (and I do mean *all* of the costs, fixed and marginal)—a matter that should bar it from further consideration until it can be resolved. It is puzzling how many opportunities to attract revenue from a variety of different models are avoided because someone believes that the core competence will be spoiled, fractured, or dishonored. My favorite example resides in the world of trade associations. Nearly all of them have enormous values that they can add to the membership but because they believe that generating income is not their core competence, they insist upon avoiding it. Cash is king.

Examples

Surprisingly, there are some high-profile examples of enterprises begun when the revenue model does *not* swamp the costs. Here are a few:

1. Anything involving solar or wind-generated power

2. Supersonic transport

3. Iridium

The Coin-Operated Laundry—Revenue Model That Swamps Costs score: 6

The model you will be using is identical to an industry that is already in existence. The challenge will be to drive your costs down so that your natural quality advantages can be adequately marketed. The innovation you are employing will not be so revolutionary as to implore a different revenue model. However, if your costs remain higher than the market will tolerate, then you should reconsider the revenue model. For example, you could consider attaching yourself to a hospital or to an association of restaurants so that you could cover all your fixed costs with your pricing for those "affiliates/partners," and hold yourself open to the public at pricing that would only need to cover your marginal costs. The "owner" clients would simply subsidize your non-owner business. Let's award this element a 6. If it weren't for the assumption about the hospital and restaurant association I would certainly award this a 2 or less. The maximum score would be reserved for an enterprise that was not burdened with a 25% cost differential above the competition.

Element 22, Revenue Model That Swamps Costs
score summary:
Weight 1 x Score 6 = Total 6

Element 23

DELIVERY ADVANTAGES

When it absolutely, positively has to be there overnight.
—Advertising theme used early in the marketing of
Federal Express overnight delivery services.

Definition

Delivery advantages include special relationships with distribution networks, low-marginal-cost delivery such as the airwaves, and other advantages not enjoyed by others in your industry. Do you have any special privileges in the distribution of your product or service that are unique to you? These can be based upon personal relationships, contractual opportunities with old friends or acquaintances, synergistic features that promote efficient piggybacking such as when the pen you manufacture could be used to fill in a golf scorecard at the U S Open PGA golf tournament, easy access to customers in

159

critical need, or an easy value add for the distribution networks already used by other suppliers or products or services that are not competing with you.

Relevance—Why Add This Element?

Delivery advantages are among the critical elements of a successful business. A delivery advantage will provide added financial cushion—you are simply a lower-cost alternative, everything else being equal. But it is also possible that the delivery advantage could be extraordinarily if not absolutely preemptive. If your delivery advantages were so overwhelming that no other competitor would be able to deliver their goods or services, then you earn a 10.

Where to Find This Answer

The first stop is the Rolodex. Do you know anyone who could provide you with a delivery advantage that can be exploited without burdensome cost or terms? If not, can you engage in some old-fashioned salesmanship to earn your product some advantage? What could you give away to win the advantage?

Score Elevation Tactics

Elevating the score can involve some basic marketing strategies devoted to the distribution sector of your business. Can you develop some form of piggybacking, special packaging, pricing incentives, commission structure, joint marketing, or other leverage that would set your product apart from the others? Think of providing bonus cash upon closing, tickets to a sporting event, an all-expense-paid round trip for two to Hawaii, an so on. Would it make sense to attach warrants for stock to your distribution agreement? Would they be good investor prospects such that they would have a sharper-than-ordinary interest in seeing you succeed?

Dr. Market's Observation:

Again, be careful here—these are excellent candidates for surprise competitors (remember our conversation about ambushes?), so a good protective agreement executed up front could be a good idea. Once you achieve a passing score, ask your lawyer to help here.

Practical Experience—This Deserves the Minimum Weight of 1

Delivery advantages can be devilish, particularly when they are actually disadvantages. The cable industry is renowned for the power wielded by the delivery mechanisms, that is, the cable owners. You can have the most compelling television programming theme ever created and if they do not allow you to distribute your programming on their channels, you are doomed. On the other hand, if they own a channel on the dial, they can then use their leverage to open another channel. Lesson? Be careful and start the process by locking down your distribution, hopefully with significant advantages.

Example

In 1980 Manny Fthenakis was managing Fairchild Telecommunications in Gaithersburg, Maryland, when Comsat, IBM, and Aetna announced the creation of Satellite Business Systems (SBS). The announcement and subsequent commitment to the new data-oriented satellite involved a lead time of at least four years to design, procure, build, test, launch, and groom the system for full data operation. Not to be outdone, Manny acquired space on satellites already in orbit, owned by AT&T. He then organized something called American Satellite Corporation and launched an aggressive sales campaign throughout the Fortune 500 where long-term contracts would allow the construction of ground segment within six months. The overwhelming majority of Manny's costs were marginal—nothing was purchased until a customer was in hand. In the mid-1980s, SBS turned up its system amid great fanfare and thundering silence in the market. It promptly went dark and the satellites were sold off to the great embarrassment of Comsat and IBM (Aetna had withdrawn long before). *USA TODAY* was one of the early users of Manny's American Satellite system.

The Coin-Operated Laundry—Delivery Advantages score: 7

Delivery advantages for this business will rely heavily upon the attributes of your location. You will score well if you are near a freeway in the center of the metropolitan area. You will score low if you are on the edge of the metropolitan area far from a freeway. You will earn a negative score if you are on the wrong side of a river with just a single two-lane bridge. Let's assume you score a 7 on this element (you could score higher if you were to have a prime location—let's see what happens with a marginal score). You will need to drive this score up, hopefully over a 9. One way to improve the score here might be to piggyback your pick-up and delivery with other pickups and deliveries around town. How about local UPS or FedEx or some other courier? Could you contract with them to do your distribution for you? What about the delivery services for the local medical labs? Might they add your chores too? Remember that they are covering your footprint with excess capacity and they might work with you to help them raise revenues without a material increase in costs. Ask around so that you can create delivery advantages for yourself.

Element 23, Delivery Advantages *score summary:*
Weight 1 x Score 7 = Total 7

Element 24

RESOURCES AVAILABLE

... enjoy to the full the resources that are within thy reach.
—*Pythian Odes*, III, 1. 109 by Pindar.

Definition

Michael Porter, the renowned professor at Harvard's Business School, has made a career out of describing the value chain, that chain of value made by adding links from the basic raw materials to your enterprise to the distribution and on to the finished product enjoyed by the consumer.[1] What resources are available that you can

---

1. Value chain is that line of production activity that proceeds from the very first element or item necessary for the creation, sale, delivery, and use of your product. It consists of links both below and above your enterprise. For a comprehensive education in matters relating to the value chain, see *http:// harvardbusinessonline.hbsp.harvard.edu* and search for "value chain."

accumulate to fulfill your value chain from end to end? More interestingly, could the availability of these resources actually become some sort of operational or financial advantage? Where are the tools necessary to make this a successful launch?

Relevance—Why Add This Element?

Can you see your needed resources now? Do you know where you will find them? If you cannot identify all the resources necessary to make this business a success, stop. You may not have much of a business. You must identify and determine the availability of all resource requirements up front. If resources are readily available, particularly in abundance, it would seem that at least half the battle to succeed is over. It could also suggest the possibility that if your product were really well crafted and well timed, a bit of seed funding could be available from one or more of the resources. Intel makes it a practice to invest seed capital in little ventures that will cause the use of lots of chips.

Where to Find This Answer

List the resources required for success and ask yourself if and how these resources will become available. Make certain that precious resources have not been co-opted, such as through long-term, exclusive contracts with the competition. Watch too for the ownership of the resources—you could find someone who owns a substitute lurking in the shareholder ranks. Worse still you might find someone who owns a critical resource that is betrothed to your competition.

Score Elevation Tactics

This is an element whose score can be elevated quickly and easily with modest market research and analysis that consume maybe an hour or two. Vendors are always prowling for purchasers and your inquiry is certain to inspire a quick response. If commitments can be made that offer sincere advantages, then this element can soar. The highest score belongs to the entrepreneur who can lock up the resources to the exclusion of all others.

> ### Dr. Market's Observation:
>
> Never go to market without backups for each element of your resource inventory.

Practical Experience—This Deserves the Maximum Weight of 3

Be prepared for surprises. This is the one area where assumptions are easy to make (certainly the vendors would love a new outlet for their products), but in a surprising number of cases the assumptions prove to be wrong. The lesson? Be careful—confirm the availability of the resources before you count them in your "win" column. In the oilfields in Russia, quite often idle resources inspire the creation of new ventures (at least within these last 10 years or so). For example, using natural gas to fuel public transportation (rather than burning it off at the well head), converting byproducts in the petroleum fields into a goo used for the repair of local roads, or using construction capabilities in oil field exploration for the creation of new public roads. These are simple resource excesses that often inspire entrepreneurial activity and advantage, based upon their easy availability. However, it has been a challenge to lock up the resources, even on a non-exclusive basis. What can seem obvious can be extremely difficult to convert into reality.

Examples

Do you have relationships with any vendors of any products or services that could be incorporated into your product or service and that can be made available to you on attractive terms? If you were trying to launch a Military Channel on cable television, would it help if a company with 100,000 hours of combat footage offered it to you for no cash for a year? Perhaps the single most important resource many of you will need to hire and outsource momentarily in the earliest moments of the venture will involve back office processing. These are the paper pushers who provide the glue to many types of business.

The Coin-Operated Laundry— Resources Available score: 7

You have a new business with new facilities and plant and you have new technology in your equipment. What assures you that you have resources available? Signed contracts and leases? How about the chemicals necessary to sustain the business? Personnel? Let's assume again that you have a marginal score, a 7. How can it be improved? The easiest way to improve this score is to not only line up the resources, but also to line up actual commitments to support you. They can be conditioned upon your funding but it is important to make certain that you are not about to be the victim of some skullduggery. Get it in writing. It's easier than you think for a vendor to commit to sell you something, so wrap your vendors up quickly. Be aware that if you encounter trouble here, you may have a real problem with a competitive block.

> ### Element 24, Resources Available *score summary:*
> Weight 3 x Score 7 = Total 21

Element 25

PREEMPTION AND
DOMINATION

Preempt: To appropriate, seize, or take for oneself before others.

Dominate: To control, govern, or rule by superior authority or power: Successful leaders dominate events rather than react to them.

Definition

Preemption is pre-positioning yourself such that others are barred from reaching the same position. You could do this by taking full ownership including possession of land—by definition you would have preempted all other ownership interests. Domination means having supremacy or preeminence over another, the exercise of mastery or ruling power, or the exercise of preponderant, governing, or controlling influence.

Relevance—Why Add This Element?

Competition is a wonderful thing...if you are on the buy side. Choices, prices, features, benefits, flexibility in terms, attentive suppliers, and the promise of life ever after flow from a lively competitive market, particularly if it is hosted by a vibrant democracy. However, if you are on the sell side, preempting and dominating a market could mean the difference between a successful business and bankruptcy. The entrepreneur must consider the possibility of preempting others from sharing the bounty of his or her idea. The higher that possibility, the more likely the company and its products will persist in the face of a determined competitor. If there are already others in the market, it is too late for preemption, but there is still a chance for domination—can the new venture dominate the market? This element indexes your chance of succeeding.

Where to Find This Answer

Any uniqueness creates the possibility of preemption and domination, and vigorous management is required to sustain the advantage. Preemption and domination should be the first element of every vision statement. They require having a mix of uniqueness and management competence. Preemption and domination, at this early moment, are little more than an approach to the entrepreneurial game. The score just now relies upon how well you believe you can succeed in preempting and dominating.

Score Elevation Tactics

To improve this score, try to forecast the establishment of irreversible advantages. Imagine improving uniquenesses and sustainability. Contemplate locking up customers, suppliers, distribution, or countries. Consider creating a new law. How can you establish protective policies? Can you piggyback your product with another whose attachment makes the conjoined products unbeatable, preemptive, and dominating? Can you give it away and catch your revenues some other way? Can you sell it to all the competitors in a large market? Can you sell it to all of the venture capitalists and bankers in existence and improve your chances in sales and in raising capital for yourself?

Practical Experience—This Deserves the Minimum Weight of 1

New ventures often succeed without being able to preempt and dominate the market. However, if you *can* preempt and dominate the market, you will stand a much greater chance of success. Note that all conversations about patents are premised upon notions of preemption and domination. If you cannot preempt and dominate your market, even if it consists of a Coin-Operated Laundry in your neighborhood, perhaps a different opportunity should be considered. Note too that preemption and domination can come and go. Once lost, there is no reason why it cannot be regained.

Dr. Market's Observation:

 Now for a sobering thought: Once your little business reaches a level of material scale, your preemption and domination could inspire some district attorney to review your compliance with antitrust laws. Be careful. In the beginning, this element is all about beefy and robust margins. In the end, this element could spell trouble. See "Game Caution" below.

Examples

Perhaps the finest example in our time is Microsoft. Preemption and dominance seem custom tailored to their growth strategy. Intelsat is or was a splendid example—actually it was set up through treaties to be preemptive and domineering. A Coca-Cola bottling franchise for a large city is also a good example.

The Coin-Operated Laundry—Preemption and Domination score: 5

You cannot preempt the cleaners market, since your competition is already in place. You will not dominate the market either, at least not for a while. The score today must be a 5 or so, and that is based upon the possibility that you could leverage your technology into such an advantage that really good, smart management on your part would drive the company into domination. Be careful as you try to muscle your way into a position of strength. Some activities may not be allowed, such as the tying of an undersold product to the sale of a popular and dominating product. This is another reason why you need a good lawyer from the very beginning.

> Element 25, Preemption and Domination *score summary:*
> Weight 1 x Score 5 = Total 5

Element 26

STRATEGY TO
PENETRATE MARKET

No wind favors him who has no destined port.
—Michel de Montaigne

Definition

Your market penetration strategy gauges the strength of your ability to successfully launch the business. The market for a new product is best viewed as hostile territory into which you must penetrate. There is not likely to be much if anything friendly about the launch. Is there a weak spot in the market that this product can attack? Is there a place where the ball can fall into fair territory? Is there a way to reach a substantial portion of your critical, irreversible market mass on day one?

175

Relevance—Why Add This Element?

This element evaluates how you propose to enter the market. It inquires about your level of clever, heads-up gamesmanship. The key is to establish your market beachhead before the opponents can react. If you can reach critical mass—that level of business activity where you cannot be pushed back out of the market—before there is adverse reaction, you will have succeeded in your launch. It would then take extraordinarily bad luck and/or poor management to cause you to squander your launch success. My favorite metaphor here is the tank and the high-explosive round or bullet the size of a beer bottle that destroys the tank by blowing it up. How did it do that? By exerting extraordinary force onto a pinpoint hole, gaining access through the five-inch hide, and spewing highly explosive heat and toxic power into the cavity it creates. Boom! Think of your launch along the lines of this phenomenon.

Where to Find This Answer

Look for large groups of customers in critical need of your products. Look for delivery advantages. Look for piggybacking candidates, particularly in high-leverage areas such as distribution when there are few distributors. Look for disgruntled customers of the competition or primary substitutes. Look for surprise opportunities to exploit. Look for ways in which your time to critical mass can be reduced.

Score Elevation Tactics

Think of ways that will make the advent of your product easier, quicker, and more irreversible. Can you create a surprise that catches the market flatfooted while you quickly reach critical mass? Can you obliterate the barriers to entry that confront you and your product? Can you partner in such a way as to position yourself for certain success? Can you piggyback your product into a market-penetrating position? Can you exploit or create some extraordinary advertising or promotion opportunity? Can you lock up a long-term relationship with sufficient charter customers or commitments to ensure critical mass? Could you receive sufficient letters of credit behind a critical mass of long-term sales, all conditioned upon delivery?

Dr. Market's Observation:

Actually, Dr. Market has two observations here: 1. Many of the tactics we use serve many masters—for example, written contracts from prospective customers up front breathe life into many of the elements and suggest that businesses can bloom almost immediately if you can lock in a customer or two. 2. There should be an enduring sense of urgency in every launch. Whenever you can move instantly to capture a moment, a deal, an opportunity, or a contract, move immediately and do not wait until tomorrow. Move, move, move, move...

Practical Experience—This Deserves the Medium Weight of 2

My best student teams solve this element prior to writing their business plans. They do it by attracting a prospect into an actual sale and then modeling their market penetration upon that first success story. On the other extreme is what we did at PTAT, the revolutionary underseas private-ownership-oriented fiber optic cable. (See Appendix II.) Our design/development/installation cycle was so long that we could not hang out in the market place for fear of losing our advantage—we were compelled to find a white knight quickly who could carry the enterprise to its next level. In the 12 months it took to locate a buyer we inspired 17 Fortune 100 companies to sign expressions of interest in our services. Naturally they were the first to sign actual purchase contracts once US Sprint took over. Penetrating the market in this case required evidence of demand that was solved with the letters from the prospective customers.

Examples

Market penetration often requires creating some advantage such as piggybacking onto an established product, using a massive discount to sell to a prominent and large-scale club, or giving away your products to 100 venture capitalists who would look for new ventures that could exploit it. The keys are spring-loading the market to accept your product or service and moving at great speed to establish yourself in the market once the spring is released.

The Coin-Operated Laundry—Strategy to Penetrate Market score: 7

Your strategy appears to be to select the right street corner, install the magic machines, and begin an aggressive marketing campaign. It is likely that you will find a suitable corner and your marketing should be sound. Let's assume that you deserve a 7. How can you improve your score? The maximum immediate irreversible customer commitment should be pursued. This goes to marketing and salesmanship. It goes to "buying" market share with pricing and incentives that may not match your total costs (please *do* try to at least cover your marginal costs). Get into business and conquer sufficient market share to avoid being pushed back into the sea.

> Element 26, Strategy to Penetrate Market *score summary:*
> Weight 2 x Score 7 = Total 14

Element 27

STRATEGY FOR
BREACHING THE CHASM

It is critical that, when crossing the chasm, you focus exclusively on achieving a dominant position in one or two narrowly bounded market segments. If you do not commit fully to this goal, the odds are overwhelmingly against your ever arriving in the mainstream market.
—Geoffrey A. Moore, *Crossing the Chasm*, Harper Business, 1991.

Definition

Geoffrey Moore's research determined that all successful new ventures must somehow negotiate their way off their beachhead. Once you have all the resources necessary to launch, can you proceed from there to broad acceptance to break even and more? Can you foresee how sales will soar after reaching some critical mass?

Relevance—why add this element?

There are several stages in converting your idea to value. This book addresses the earliest: conception. Ultimately you hope to build a wonderful enterprise that creates many jobs and great personal wealth for the shareholders. Along the way you first must win seed funding, then first-round funding, then launch, and so forth. Imagine that you have successfully penetrated the market and you are at critical mass—you cannot easily be pushed out of the market. However, before you can reach the last plateau that leads you toward harvest, you must inspire a broad sector of the customer profile to purchase your product or service. You must breach the chasm that often exists between the successful launch and the land of lengthening margins, break even, and talk of harvest. The question here is this: what is your strategy for this maneuver? Note the dynamics of consumer products versus products destined for other businesses (often called "B2B," as in business to business). There is a temptation to view this element as relevant only to consumer products. However, it applies to all kinds of products. It is often possible to foresee how you will breach the chasm within the first moments of an idea's existence, and this is where you score that forecast.

Where to Find This Answer

This element is far into the future. However, you should be able to sense today how this could play out. The logical zone for consideration is marketing. Review the following for possible ways to discover your "breaching the chasm" potential:

1. Perception: Can the perception of your product be adjusted for broad appeal?

2. Pitch: Can you pitch your product for broad appeal?

3. Packaging: Can your packaging lend itself to enduring use and acceptance?

4. Price: Can the price adjust itself to long-term appeal?

5. Promotion: Can you promote this product in a broad array of media?

6. Promises: Can you make promises that will attract a broad customer base?

7. Piggybacking: Can you piggyback your product onto a number of other products that makes yours ubiquitous?

8. Positioning: Can you position your product for extraordinary lift in the market after your launch?

9. Placement: Can you place your product into a market sector that soars into broad acceptance?

10. Premiums: Can a campaign of premiums result in broad appeal?

11. Publicity: Can sufficient publicity be built to promote broad appeal?

12. Perseverance: Will simple perseverance sustain your breach of the chasm?

Score Elevation Tactics

Examine the elements described above. There are clues in that list regarding how you will breach the chasm and therefore how you should score this element.

Practical Experience—This Deserves a Modest Weight of 1

You should be able to see how you will broaden your market quite early in the analysis of your idea. Prospective investors will also need to see how the future is almost certain to unfold. It is particularly helpful to plan on this element at the outset so that the enterprise can be properly aligned to reach its objectives.

Dr. Market's Observation:

Before you write your business plan you should have a solid answer for this element. Now, today, as you contemplate your idea, you should already have an idea about what you intend to do to breach the chasm.

Examples

If you are a software manufacturer, embed your product in all new PC computers sold. If your product is useful in automobiles, have it installed in all new cars. If it is a cosmetic product, try to have it used by all NFL cheerleaders. If it is a consumer product with repetitive sales, give it away to all graduating seniors at colleges across the country. If your product can make the products or services of entire industries more effective and efficient, make certain that the capital markets are aware of it, perhaps by your giving samples of it away.

The Coin-Operated Laundry—Strategy for Breaching the Chasm score: 7

This is the next challenge after you have established a successful market penetration. You will move from early adopters to majority users in the market. How do you do it? Forecast this maneuver now, up front. Let's say you have predicted that you will employ long-term, large-scale contracts and that you will exploit every cost-reducing opportunity at your disposal. Let's further assume that you can award your enterprise with a score of 7. How can it be improved? Remember that breaching the chasm for this enterprise will mean the events of about year 5 and thereafter. An important tactic therefore could be in becoming, today, the cleaners of first choice for every high-school kid in the region. Stay with them through college, even if that place is far away. When it comes time for you to breach the chasm you will find yourself and the company to be the cleaner of choice for the coming generation. Naturally, the most obvious way to breach the chasm is to multiply your locations and then drive the marketing and promotion. At some point you might use all the various outlets as drivers for an operation that expands to speciality cleaning, pressing, and finished products.

> Element 27, Strategy for Breaching the Chasm
> *score summary:*
> Weight 1 x Score 7 = Total 7

Element 28

PROPRIETARY
OWNERSHIP

*No horse gets anywhere until he is harnessed. No steam or gas
ever drives anything until it is confined. No Niagara is ever
turned into light and power until it is tunneled. No life ever grows
great until it is focused, dedicated, disciplined.*
—Harry Emerson Fosdick, D.D.

Definition

Can the idea be bottled and sold under your ownership? Or is it an
idea that defies such exclusive possession, something that cannot be
parsed out from your shelves at a price over which you have
control? If you go to the effort of changing a law in Washington,[1]
can you end up with the lion's share of the winnings from the
change without violating the Constitution? Can you attach enough
value to the idea that people who wish to own or use the product or

---

1. The same goes for all legislative bodies—federal, state, county, and city.

service think first and foremost of you? Can you possess the product or service to the exclusion of all others? Can you control its release in doses required by the paying customers? Can you determine whether there are any barriers to entry to your newly established market?

Relevance—Why Add This Element?

Many ideas flow through the entrepreneur's fingers—too often there is no way to catch the lightning and put it into your bottle. An inability to possess and therefore to control the solution to a critical unserved need means that your costs could easily exceed your revenues, a feature that will doom your enterprise from the start. To the extent you can actually own the solution or a piece of it, you will be able to gain sufficient traction to succeed through launch to harvest. This element scores your ability to bottle the lightning.

Where to Find This Answer

Important clues on ownership come from your ability to patent, copyright, or trademark the essence of the idea. Failing that, could there be some barrier for copycat competitors erected by the government, distributors, suppliers, or a customer user group that would make copying and marketing prohibitively expensive? Is there any exclusive deal through which you could sell your products or services? Is there any barrier that would prevent copycat products from reaching a prospective customer if you activated the barrier and said no?

Score Elevation Tactics

If you own little or nothing that can be mixed, processed, bottled, and sold with your name affixed, you must stop all conversations until you elevate your score. Tactics include adding substance to the product or service that *can* be owned. If you are about to launch a business by offering a product that others give away, you must add something to the mix that you can own, something special that only you can possess and sell.

Practical Experience—This Deserves the Maximum Weight of 3

Erin Dolezal of Danube, Minnesota, pointed out that if we were to succeed in winning the rights to license defunct broadcast frequencies for use by Internet purveyors, we would not be able to bottle up the rights so that we could own something valuable. She was absolutely correct, and reminded me that an up front question for all ventures is whether they can create a product that can be bottled up and sold. If there is development work for your launch, will you be solving puzzles for your competition such that they have no work to do in order to compete with you? Have you created an automatic cost advantage for your competition?

Examples

Ownership means you have the ability to "just say no." If you cannot say no to someone using something, you don't own it. Here are some troublesome things that are difficult to own or control: the ether (unless the FCC can license your use), opinions, the weather, or any other matter, tangible or intangible, where it is impossible to stop others from using or selling the same thing. Gatekeepers must exist because you must be able to prevent others from using your product without paying for the privilege.

The Coin-Operated Laundry—Proprietary Ownership score: 5

Since you are simply buying machinery for your enterprise, you are not able to bottle up the access to the availability of the process. I give it a 5 to account for the possibility that you might be able to acquire some protection via franchise or license that would include territorial exclusivity. This element needs attention upon your review.

> Element 28, Proprietary Ownership *score summary:*
> Weight 3 x Score 5 = Total 15

Element 29

PARTNERING
CANDIDATES

Getting along with others is the essence of getting ahead, success being linked with cooperation.
— William Feather

Definition

Can this business be a candidate for partnering with a firm or institution that could be trusted not to swallow it? Could this partnering make sense in penetration of the market or in breaching the chasm? Could the partner be in fact a huge customer, vendor, or distributor? Even if you never close with a partner, is one visible up front just in case you need to move quickly?

Relevance—Why Add This Element?

A partner offers you a significant expansion of options as you approach your launch. Reduction of risk is therefore the key to this element. It is particularly useful for your partner to be a firm or institution(s) that will not swallow you with an offer you cannot refuse. You thus gain access to a customer base otherwise not available in a straight, unadorned attempt to launch your product. Attracting a high-value partner also can have a significant impact upon the amount of equity you must surrender to attract your funding—it creates instant value that will reduce the amount of equity needed to attract the same amount of money.

Dr. Market's Observation:

Remember, this Partnering Candidates element simply calculates the *potential* for attracting a great partner; it does not force you to actually follow through (yet)! It's a wedge against failure.

Where to Find This Answer

Look for frailty or weakness in your company or product that can be solved with a big partner, possibly a charter customer. Be careful to avoid partners who might some day devour you.[1] Examine most closely the distribution networks looking toward the potential for

---

1. Big partners are two-edged swords. They certainly can be invaluable in conquering some market dragon. However, they can also be used to cut your company in two. Partners learn all about your business and if they like your business, they can simply wait for the right opportunity and then "assist" you with finance or other resources that will cause you to sacrifice control to them.

piggybacking. With any good fortune you will find a superb partner who offers you the opportunity to grow in a number of directions while at the same time allowing you to exploit *their* customers. Partnering offers marketing advantages to firmly establish your business and carry it into and past break even.

Score Elevation Tactics

Strive for value-chain candidates who might see the advantages of working with you. Forward and backward integration can be keys to success in elevating your score. Look in the distribution ranks for products that would gain by your success. You can also look for large-scale customers whose massive purchases can drive market share for your products—a sure indicator of synergistic selling. Examine your upstream resource vendors who themselves could drive expanded sales of their products that you consume.

Practical Experience—This Deserves the Minimum Weight of 1

Partnering Candidates is a defensive element that involves attracting a big brother who can do your fighting for you. It can save the venture from extinction but it also invites a kind of predatory cooperation by the big partner. In other words, I am not a fan of partnering, even though I recognize that it might prove necessary. The reason for my concern is the difference in scale and profitability between the partner and the startup. If there is balance, then you have a good candidate for longevity. If not, you may have a carnivorous act waiting for the right time. Be careful here.

Examples

Perhaps the most remarkable, day-after-day partnership program involves the federal government purchasing system that awards advantages to minority- and woman-owned businesses. The vast majority of the purchases found at *www.eps.gov/spg/index.html* are open to proposals from one of these firms. Almost none are qualified on their own to win any of this business because they are stacked up against industry titans with literally tens of thousands of employees and billions of dollars in cash on the balance sheet— lots of luck competing with that when you are a little newbie.[2] However, if they can attract the support of a partner with a name and set of resources widely recognized by the federal government, then they can win the business on the strength of their minority/woman-owned advantage and the resources of the large partner. As a matter of fact, you should always learn whether the government (state, local, and federal) could use your products. If so, find the right type of partner that would help assure you of winning the business and chase the opportunity.

The Coin-Operated Laundry—Partnering Candidates score: 8

At this early stage, the Partnering Candidates question applies to a firm that you can see would or could own a portion of your company such that you have a greater chance of success. The easy possibility is the hospital or the restaurant association. The score

---

2. If you are intrigued, look into the weight and bearing of Science Applications International Corporation (SAIC) in doing business with the federal government. The government (state governments often have lookalike counterparts) is trying to "level the playing field."

here should easily be an 8 *if* you can foresee with whom you would partner. Improvement in the score would involve finding a large and dominating customer or working with a strong and fair-minded resource such as the manufacturer. You might preempt the potential here by actually raising the franchising issue. One ploy might be to actually purchase the machines with a proviso in the contract that in the event of conversion to franchise, you would receive a free pass on the up-front franchise fee. This would put you into business automatically.

> Element 29, Partnering Candidates *score summary:*
> Weight 1 x Score 8 = Total 8

Element 30

APPROPRIATENESS OF LOCATION

In the theater of confusion, knowing the location of the exits is what counts.
—Mason Cooley, U S aphorist. *City Aphorisms*,
Fifth Selection, New York, 1988.

Definition

Typically, the location of the enterprise coincides with the home of the entrepreneur or, at this earliest of moments, you, the person with the idea. However there are other factors that should come into play, particularly factors such as talent pools, customer location, distribution networks, and supplier outlets, all of which should influence this element heavily.

> ### Dr. Market's Observation:
>
> The key is where the enterprise is best situated for *success*. You can always return home after you harvest the enterprise. (*Psst*: This means don't sell the house just yet.)

Relevance—Why Add This Element?

The wrong location diminishes the potential for success. As is often the case with elements in the Scorecard, a high score translates to lower costs. Despite the location of the idea person, there are sometimes only a few places where an idea can attract the resources that will be the key to success.

Where to Find This Answer

Appropriateness of Location is among the easier elements to evaluate because you know where your customers, distributors, suppliers, and talent pools are situated geographically. The University of North Dakota in Grand Forks is not a hotbed of action in software or computer chip manufacture. However, in aviation, energy, nutrition, and biological study, it can be second to none. The lesson here is that if the idea is aligned with the strengths of the community, it should score well in location appropriateness.

Score Elevation Tactics

Boosting this score can involve a change of venue or somehow multiplying the centers of activity. Determine the true nature of the resources available in your location now—your community could have the "right stuff" after all. It is also helpful to remember that the enterprise can move once it has been groomed for launch. However, after the first day you are open for business, it becomes increasingly more and more difficult to move. Also, the center of gravity for your customers, vendors, distributors, and talent can shift, and you could be compelled to move with them.

Practical Experience—This Deserves the Medium Weight of 2

It seems that no place is ever perfect. I have worked in North Dakota with plenty of seed capital waiting for opportunities, plenty of ideas, a fine university, and extremely close relationships with both US senators and the local congressman. However, it is a tough location because the talent pool is thin and the markets are all far, far away. I have also worked in the Washington DC area where we had plenty of talented people, universities, and ideas, but little seed capital. My recommendation is that you find a location where the resources you most require to succeed are in plentiful supply and then build around it. Note that if you are contemplating a business that relies heavily upon distributing information on the Internet and via the telephone, and if you have long hoped to live in a particular setting, such as in the South near the water and a golf course, now might be the time to initiate your conversations with people there who might support your venture

Don't use cost savings as an excuse for a location that handicaps or even dooms the enterprise. Low costs of living and low costs of labor in a remote location might be tempting, especially if you already live there. After all, the Internet and Federal Express solve remoteness and allow companies to flourish wherever the entrepreneurial spirit blooms. But be careful. My favorite example here was a manager's insistence that video production of a cable channel devoted to the military should be situated in a river town in the Midwest. Never mind that Washington, DC, about 550 miles to the east, was a 24/7 marketing opportunity for all aspects of the enterprise. In that case the costs of not being in Washington were staggering and insurmountable. The network failed in that town— twice, once before chapter 11 and once afterward. The point? Location as a cost reduction bonus is often trumped by location as a strategic marketing, talent pool, and business-accumulating bonus.

Dr. Market's Observation:

 Many communities simply do not have highly talented legal expertise in seed capital negotiation and contracting, intellectual property protection, or other highly sophisticated matters relating to launching and growing new businesses. Do not be surprised if your "right firm" with the requisite skills is far away, possibly in another state. By using the big, out-of-state firm, you win their expertise, they would have few conflicts of interest, and there is an automatic expansion possibility into their headquarters location—they would make it very easy for you.[1]

Examples

Some of the tightest location matches go to the following:

1. Software and Silicon Valley.

2. Biomedical and Maryland and San Diego.

---

1. There will never be a substitute for the local law firm for local legal matters such as property, zoning, contract litigation, local torts, etc

3. Pico-engineering and Ithaca, New York.

4. Search tools and Minneapolis (remember the gopher?).

5. Defense and Washington, D.C.

6. Media and New York City.

The Coin-Operated Laundry— Appropriateness of Location score: 8

Your business here is overwhelmingly dependent upon your location. You or your customers are moving cleaning between their homes or shops and your cleaning establishment(s). It is assumed that you will be a retail commercial enterprise that cleans clothing and other fabric. You therefore need to situate your plant at the optimum address. Let's score this as an 8 on the assumption that you can find a real estate agent worth his or her salt. How could you improve the score? Multiply the locations and lease rather than buy the premises so that you can always move if the location proves mediocre.

> Element 30, Appropriateness of Location *score summary:*
> Weight 2 x Score 8 = Total 16

Element 31

QUALITY OF THE BACKUP PLAN

*Daring ideas are like chessmen moved forward; they may be
beaten, but they may start a winning game.*
—Johann Wolfgang von Goethe

Definition

Once you're launched, the investor's money is committed to the
venture. It is at full risk. Or is it? Could there be a hedge that would
allow a less-grandiose scheme, lower in risk and yet capable of
appreciable gain? This is the backup plan you use if your primary
path becomes blocked.

Relevance—Why Add This Element?

Quality of the Backup Plan is a confidence builder for the entrepreneur and for the investors. Typically, when people think about an investment, they dwell on the upside. How high can this go? However, after a devastating surprise, what could be left of the investment? Could anything be saved? The key here is creating a downward sticky investment opportunity for the investor—make it so the investment will not go down too far. The upside is well understood by all. Here is the opportunity to demonstrate that the odds of losing the investment are somehow restricted, slowed, or reduced to nil. A solid backup plan will reassure the investor who is considering your idea, and now is a good time to give it some thought, right up front.

Dr. Market's Observation:

 Frankly, it is not impossible that the original direction ends up being a decoy or diversion for your competition or opponents while the real enterprise is protected from harm's way. In other words, you might be able to protect your idea from your opponents by disguising it as your backup.

Where to Find This Answer

Watch for any other modest revenue stream that could be achieved without major added capital commitments. To what could your launch assets be reduced or diverted? Must it be inside the country? If you manufacture metal automobile bumpers, can you divert quickly into the manufacture of cooking pots (the All-Clad story)? If the anti-fog headlight business proved unworthy, could you divert the resources into, say, a business that would be reliant upon another type of light diffraction, such as photography (the Polaroid story)?

Score Elevation Tactics

Your business could survive on a much more limited basis. Look for areas that could be peeled off and positioned for a generous revenue stream in a separate and distinct direction—it might not cover the entire nut but it could offer some breathing room until the next (and inevitable) opportunity to expand came your way. You might also find alternative uses for your products, or substantial portions of your products. There is always a potential for overseas distribution of your products in countries none of your competitors have yet reached—in this case you might be able to preempt and dominate your competition overseas.

Dr. Market's Observation:

You may be able to subcontract to your competition, in a sense turning them into your partner, particularly overseas. Stranger things have happened on the way to robust harvests.

Practical Experience—This Deserves the Minimum Weight of 1

As the late Alvin George Flanagan of Combined Communications Corporation and later Gannett Broadcasting Group told us, "don't ever get caught without a backup plan." You simply never know when a surprise will turn your company upside down. Frankly, I have witnessed surprises on the positive side as well, so I do not believe that the backup plan needs to be a doomsday scenario. The point is that you should plan on both types of backup scenario, certainly on the negative when things go bad, and also on the positive if things go wildly beyond your expectations.[1]

Examples

Some possible backups include:

1. Distributing defense-related programming accumulated by a military-themed cable programmer to other cable channels if adequate distribution is not possible.

2. Selling fiber optic capacity to a large carrier if you cannot break up and sell the capacity on a smaller, fractionalized, and higher-margin basis.

Dr. Market's Observation:

 If something should be working but it's not, is there a gender, race, religion, orientation, or political issue in the air? Can your backup plan maneuver you around the problem?

---

1. This is a slightly different way of examining extraordinary growth and the solution is often outsourcing and temporary partnering until added permanent resources can be brought on line.

The Coin-Operated Laundry—Quality of the Backup Plan score: 3

We have already spoken about partnering in an emergency. What will you do if this business simply refuses to lift off? What is the quality of your plan? A Coin-Operated Laundry with an accompanying cleaners is not easy to back up. My sense is that this element should score low, a 3. How could we raise the score? We could sell the cleaning side to a competitor and retain an outlet status in the Coin-Operated Laundries. If your lawyer had been clever, you would be able to return the machines if the competition were too strong or if the manufacturer sold into your territory. You might then create a more traditional Coin-Operated Laundry with more competitive prices. Another possibility is to create a bazaar of sorts with a consignment setup—third-party cleaners would operate through your premises, Western Union would operate a money transfer business, a check cashing franchise could operate there, and a photography processing operation could be installed. Finally, tap the Internet[2] and determine if there might be assets you could acquire for a nickel on the dollar and position in your premises for a consignment type of business.

> Element 31, Quality of Backup Plan *score summary:*
> Weight 1 x Score 3 = Total 3

---

2. For example see: *www.bankruptcysales.com/home.asp*

Element 32

UNFAIR ADVANTAGES

There is always inequality in life. Some men are killed in a war and some men are wounded and some men never leave the country. Life is unfair.
—John Fitzgerald Kennedy, U.S. president. Press conference, March 21, 1962.

Definition

Some might view your advantages as unfair. Not illegal, mind you. Just unfair. These matters tend to be personal in nature and the more secretive and unknown, the more potent the advantage. For example, if you were to seek to compete with an international telecommunications cartel there would certainly be an advantage in having the pro-active support of the president of the United States of America. Would obtaining that support be legal? Assuming that there were no untoward financial involvement, sure. Would it be fair? That depends on whose side you are on.

209

Relevance—Why Add This Element?

It is astounding what happens when you own unfair advantages. They can assert themselves at any point in the value chain. They can be advantages in government relations, in securing a key vendor or distributor, and even in being a respected image held in the minds of the customers. Magical results can occur, laws can be changed, nations can be swayed, banks can join in your funding, distribution for your competition can suddenly collapse, and customers can make all their purchases in your favor. This element measures the height, weight, passion, ubiquity, and raw power of the guerrilla in your closet (your unfair advantage).

Where to Find This Answer

The more obvious or open your advantage, the less advantageous it will be. Once the secret is out, it is easy to deploy blocking resources against you or the person delivering the advantage to you. So the unfairness is in direct proportion to the secrecy and the prominence of the person delivering or providing the advantage. An unfair advantage is typically not disclosed in the business plan. You may not even know you have it, but if you do, be very quiet about it. You can score yourself high but you should not be touting it. Mum's the word.

Score Elevation Tactics

Can you find a politically powerful friend who can throw his or her weight around the market without being too obvious? The more invisible the support, the higher the potential for very serious value to the venture. Another approach is to somehow attract a person who is dreadfully conflicted but who would find your success to be quite valuable to their business (or political career). For example, could you inspire a lawyer to drop helpful remarks in support of you despite the fact that his or her clients were aligned against you?

Practical Experience—This Deserves the Maximum Weight of 3

There are two elements that appear to be slightly wacky and this is one of them (the other one is Pretending Not to Know, Element 40). It is top secret because otherwise your advantage will be compromised by your opponents. However, there is nothing quite like it. I actually lived through the ultimate Unfair Advantage. Ward L. Quaal of the *Chicago Tribune* (former chairman) stopped by our office in Washington shortly after we had filed the application for our Orion to compete with Intelsat. He introduced himself and explained how proud he and his friend "Dutch" were to see us attempting to tackle a 130-nation international satellite cartel. His only request? Please let him know if there were any problems so that he and his friend could do what they could to help. We later learned the identity of "Dutch" but the people from Intelsat never discovered our secret. In mid September of 1985, a little over two years after we filed the application, the FCC granted us a license that set the stage for us to compete in all respects with the cartel. Thank you, again, Mr. Quaal, and thank you, Mr. President. Note that the advantage can materialize at any time, so be on the prowl.

Examples

Obviously the ultimate unfair advantage example is what happened at Orion—the quiet, energetic, and enthusiastic support of the president of the United States. We also enjoyed other "unfair" advantages at Orion. Early in the campaign we attracted the attention of a brilliant French diplomat and economist named Dr. Odile Sarcy Chapman, who orchestrated the unanimous support of all 33 nations of the world whose official language is French. Her concern was the incredible expense of moving electronic communications traffic between those countries, particularly in a competitive game with countries who used other languages such as English. Other examples could be doing business in the Czech Republic with Czech partners who were once members of the Czech intelligence agency, or doing business with a company that owns more than 80% of a country's media.

Dr. Market's Observation:
If this element is weighted a 3 (the max) and you score a zero, what should you do? Go find an unfair advantage.

The Coin-operated Laundry—Unfair Advantages score: 2

You cannot score this item higher than a 2 unless you can co-opt some huge decision maker to quietly ensure that an enormous amount of business goes your way (no bribing allowed, but lawful compensation or countertrade can be fair game). This can mean chatting up the key decision makers in areas that could make your business a huge success. You need them to support you quietly, without divulging their enthusiasm (such a disclosure could make their views vulnerable to reversal).

> ### Element 32, Unfair Advantages *score summary:*
> Weight 3 x Score 2 = Total 6

FINANCE

Introduction

Financing may be farther away in your future than any of the elements in the preceding sections. However there are some issues you should address now, such as the source and type of funding you will need. Let's look at how manageable your requirements are, whether you can keep your burn rate low until launch, and where you see yourself finding the necessary funds.

Element 33

MANAGEABLE CAPITAL REQUIREMENTS

If capital an' labor ever do git t'gether
it's good night fer th' rest of us.
—Saying of entertainer Frank McKinney "Kin"
Hubbard, aka Abe Martin.

Definition

There's no question you will need capital to launch your business. Whether your capital requirements are manageable is another question. Note that the penalty for having non-manageable capital requirements, assuming that you plow ahead, is time. It just takes longer to find the right source, conform the deal to their needs, make the case, and close. Note, though, that raising $100 million is a different challenge from raising $6 million. It is not likely that the venture investment community will bet $100 million on a new venture without extraordinary reassurance that the value will

217

someday return home. Furthermore, $100 million is likely to easily exceed one of the principles of the investor—avoiding placing too many dollars into one basket. Large investment requirements are normally syndicated or spread amongst several investment pools.

Relevance—Why Add This Element?

Manageable Capital Requirements represents the impact of the capital markets' willingness to embrace your enterprise. Among other things, large-scale capitalization requires verification that the product or service will be compelling, that no ambush will be awaiting the launch, and that management is certain to stay the course and win. There may also be pressure to move the capitalization process off-shore, where tax benefits can be exploited. This pressure can work in your favor; the market offshore could be more compliant with your requirements than the domestic market.

Dr. Market's Observation:

 On the low end, other problems can loom. It can be difficult to find small levels of capital commitment if the investors feel that the launch will *not* be followed by a dramatic upward swing in valuation that would sustain attractive later-round financing. At this tender early moment, plan on seeking what you require to reach break even and anticipate the challenges you will face in attracting that sum of money. If you will not be requiring any capital from investors (other than your family), award yourself a 10.

Multiple-round financing packages are difficult to manage unless they are organized up front in anticipation of the upcoming rounds. Investors loathe downside surprises and if you cannot break even before your next round, you have not managed your capital program well. The result will be traumatic for the early investors who will take out their frustrations on you—you can say goodbye to your stake in the company. The key to a good campaign is to seek capital only when you appear not to need it, just like a line of credit from a commercial bank.

You are likely to have only two free bites at the apple. One will be the seed round and the second will be the first round. From then on you must manage your campaign from the high ground of a successful enterprise—undertake further capital rounds following operational break even. If you cannot foresee today how this can be accomplished, you may be asking for heartache and a mediocre personal financial reward.

Let's pause to consider funding the wildly successful enterprise that for its first six years posts a 100%+ increase in revenues each year. This is the "Brian" story (Brian was one of my students). It became evident that the investors would do quite well in Brian's company,[1] but nowhere near as well as they would if they could pump up their equity. They have attempted to convince management that the company requires added cash, a ploy too transparent for management to bite. There is now fear that the investors might actually harm the company in their quest for a bigger stake.

Where to Find This Answer

While the logic is slightly circular, if the management is solid, if the story is punchy and compelling, if the product is sustainably

---

1. I'm avoiding naming the company to protect the guilty.

unique, and if there are no showstoppers, and so forth, then the capital needs can be manageable. Note however that any seed capital requirements in excess of $10 million are likely to be problematic. If the capital is serious and therefore from a zone often occupied by professional investors, a high aggregate score on the Scorecard should drive a high score on this element. Give this a moment's thought: if your aggregate score is very high, say a 90% without this element's score, it is likely that you are quite attractive to the investment community and will be able to award yourself a high grade on this element.

Score Elevation Tactics

It is tempting to counsel moderation. The less money required, the more likely you are to receive it. You may also receive your funding if you appear not to need it. But as is often the case in new venture launching, the reverse could be closer to the truth: It could just be easier to raise a whopping amount of money than it is to raise just a little bit. If this score is low, it could be best to first address the management team issue—that is the first place your investors will look. Fifty million dollars for a new software venture could be unreasonable unless it is discovered that the prospective CEO of this new company is Bill Gates. Once the management has been reviewed, then it could make sense to determine a more rational capitalization scheme, say, less than $10 million until the concept could be proven for sure. To keep management that is most likely to deliver a success, investors will sometimes be quick to make special concessions to the team.

While we are on the subject of management solving a low score on capitalization requirements, here is another tactic. Try to position all executives so that their financial requirements will be met by other means, at least until either break even or substantial capital infusion. This could occur by all hands receiving retirement checks or holding jobs not on their résumés, such as night shift at the factory, driving a cab, running a subway train, and the like. Just smile and keep moving, knowing that better days are waiting. This could drive your capitalization score up and solve your management questions at the same time.

Practical Experience—This Deserves the Maximum Weight of 3

My experience with raising funds is that it is never easy and you often do not receive enough to carry you to the next round. The key is to keep the capital requirements manageable and dwell on achieving operational break even at the earliest practicable time. Orion and PTAT were telecommunications projects, each of which required hundreds of millions of dollars. Each one had its own unique challenges with the up-front fund raising.

If you pay attention up front to reducing the capital required for your enterprise, you might be surprised what you can do for yourself. Companies with yawning capital requirements sometimes solve them with clever and patient brick-by-brick accumulation of capital, risk-reducing measures, and short-term backup plans for generating revenue using other people's resources.

Today the venture capital market is staggering from burdens created during the great run-up of the late 1990s and 2000. It is attempting to fight its way up the food chain toward reduced-risk investing, much like investment banking. You should familiarize yourself with such terms as "participating preferred," "liquidation preferences," and "full ratchet."[2] If you can understand them now,

---

2. See "Venture Capitalists Are Taking the Gloves Off," New York Times, Sunday, July 28, 2002, page four in the Business Section, by Lynnley Browning. These tactics are not new, however, and have been floating around the market for years.

and if you can acknowledge that your enterprise really should be self-funded as much as possible, then this Innovator's Scorecard will save you enormous sums of grief and heartburn.

Examples

There are a small number of businesses that can be launched with relatively little if any capital. Consulting is probably the premiere example, although that would require overlooking the sunk costs of the education and training. Furthermore, if you have a hot market, your capital requirements might be capable of being marginalized (i.e., capital required only if there is a sale), as they were in the Y2K situation mentioned earlier.

The Coin-Operated Laundry— Manageable Capital Requirements score: 8

Are you tackling a highly innovative, technologically sophisticated idea that requires heavy research and even heavier capitalization? Not really. You are buying some special laundry equipment and leasing a building. It's just not very challenging when it comes to the capital required and I would award it an 8. If you do find that you are confronting a $100 million + capital nut, make certain that your expenditures drive the cost of entry up by some multiple so that you can enjoy uniquenesses that are unassailable. Furthermore, if you are in this situation, stop. Ask yourself if the capitalization can be so broken up and prioritized that it can become manageable. If not, assign this element a –10 because it will actually be working against you, to the maximum.

> Element 33, Manageable Capital Requirements
> *score summary:*
> Weight 3 x Score 8 = Total 24

Element 34

LOW CASH REQUIRED
BEFORE LAUNCH

There are no intrinsic reasons for the scarcity of capital.
—John Maynard Keynes, *The General Theory of Employment, Interest and Money*, 1936.

Definition

In contrast to the previous element, which relates to the total capital requirement, Low Cash Required Before Launch is limited to what happens prior to launch. It is often related to accumulating resources and knocking down risks prior to the commitment of launch capital and the follow through. Low prelaunch cash required is possible if during the prelaunch period, when a low level of capital is consumed, you can also greatly reduce your risks. As you accumulate the resources required to launch, can you minimize (if not eliminate altogether) your burn rate, that is, the rate by which you burn cash?

223

Relevance—Why Add This Element?

Low Cash Required Before Launch measures whether you are likely to win an opportunity to approach a launch. Few new ventures can launch with just one round of fundraising. The first key stage will be the positioning for actual launch with a modest amount of cash (often called the seed round); the next round, often called the first round, can be arranged only after a significant reduction of risk. With this first round of capital you should have enough customer demand to pull the enterprise through the difficult launch phase. Note however that while important, raising the next round during the launch can be so distracting to management that a successful launch is threatened. The compromise is to stage the capital so that if certain milestones are achieved, the next round is automatic.

Where to Find This Answer

Looking out over the resources you need to assemble and commit, to what extent can all your cash commitments be marginalized so that they are payable only after a sale is made? From another slightly different perspective, how much of the first round capital can cover costs that have been postponed until after the seed round?

Score Elevation Tactics

To raise this score, you might consider postponing cash obligations past the launch date. Can you foresee how you can drive your costs into the zone past the actual launch? Never pay today what can be postponed until the day after tomorrow. If cash is king, horde it and don't surrender it to anyone until after you are confident you will receive more.

Dr. Market's Observation:

One important clue is the strength of the IPO[1] market. If investors and senior management see that they will be able to cash out when the company goes public, the pace of capitalization events will pick up—the phones will ring and people will want to do your fundraising deal. If the IPO market is strong, there will be a ripple effect all the way down to the entry level where you will be playing. Costs are easier to postpone if the IPO market is robust because your investors and management team will all be reassured about the proximity of their payday.

Practical Experience—This Deserves the Medium Weight of 2

The longer you can postpone serious cash commitments the more likely you are to fund the venture through its early risk-reducing phases out of your own pocket. In tight financial markets, this may be critical to your success.

I am tempted to report that scale is not as relevant as careful attention to this element of the Scorecard. Can a solo human being with no money of his or her own build a dam across a major river? Sure. However, to succeed, that person will need to keep a roof over his or her head and carefully piece together the partnering commitments prior to the moment when the real, cash-consuming work needs to be done. Christopher Columbus did not underwrite the costs for the ships, equipment, supplies, and people necessary for the voyage to America. He sold the Queen on the idea and *she*

---

1. An IPO is an initial public offering, and it results in shares of stock becoming "registered" so that they can be sold and purchased on a public market such as NASDAQ.

underwrote the trip. He ramped up the project with little or nothing and she paid the big bills when they were due.

By the way, every dime you spend today on your idea can come home to you, but only in stock or at harvest and rarely otherwise. Don't count on having your loans to the company being paid off in cash before harvest. New investors do not like it prior to harvest.

Examples

Any *successful* venture, really, works to validate this point about keeping prelaunch cash expenditures low. SBS and Iridium both spent enormous sums of cash prior to launch, and both failed. Orion and PTAT both sipped at the capital trough until their risks had been reduced, and only *then* did their serious capital consumption begin, matched with the capital they had lined up. They both succeeded. Perhaps the lesson is that you really may not have to spend much money at all to bring the right idea to market. Exceptions to the rule? Media. If you are trying to crack a certain number of viewers or readers in broadcast TV or cable TV, the rough rule of thumb is $100 million and 10 years to break even.

The Coin-Operated Laundry—Low Cash Required Before Launch score: 8

You are launching a new business that provides cleaner and Coin-Operated Laundry services. The important thing is to lease the space, acquire possession of the equipment, hire the staff, and initiate service. How should this be scored? Normally this element is calculated to anticipate an innovation that involves significant capital that we are hoping, in this element, to postpone as far as possible. Let's award you with an 8 just to keep moving through the Scorecard. How can it be improved? Bump every possible obligation into the status of marginal cost, that is, make them payable only upon receipt of cash. Obliterate cash outlays as much as possible prior to launch. Make every possible expenditure conditional upon the launch. No launch, no exposure.

Element 34, Low Cash Required Prelaunch
score summary:
Weight 2 x Score 8 = Total 16

Element 35

VISIBLE CAPITAL

Every man...is left perfectly free to bring both his industry and capital into competition with those of any other man or order of men.
—Adam Smith, *An Inquiry into the Nature and Causes of the Wealth of Nations*, chapter 9, 1776.

Definition

It is not that you can actually "see" the money, but rather whether you can visualize where you might find it. Angel money? Venture capital? Corporate funding? Overseas funding? Government grant? Where is the money that would be interested in your success at this early moment? Is it smart money or is it dumb?

Relevance—Why Add This Element?

Aside from the obvious, the real import of the Visible Capital element is the confidence provided by its presence. Frankly, no capital is truly visible until someone at the bank calls with the news that the funds have cleared. However, the score on this element can be useful when anticipating the challenges of raising money. Who can you approach for your capital? Is there direct access to any angels or investment firms who understand this business? If there is access to such individuals or firms, then your fundraising campaign should move along toward closure. If not, then you could find that this opportunity takes more time to fund than you can tolerate.

Where to Find This Answer

For a new entrepreneur, "seeing" your capital can be a challenge. Here is the best way to get a 7 on this score: find a copy of the current *Pratt's Guide to Venture Capital Sources*,[1] most likely available in a good local library, and certainly available on *www.amazon.com*. While pricey (new is over $600 and used is about 1/6 of the new purchase price), it is rich with names and contact information of the firms that have experience in your general area of expertise. Also name the individuals who have profited tremendously by investing in your industry. They are the "smart" investors who will later find the right capital resources to further assure that their investment comes home. Who are these people?

---

1. Stanley E. Pratt, *Pratt's Guide to Venture Capital 2002*. Venture Economics, 2002.

Score Elevation Tactics

Beware the need to maintain confidentiality—don't go blathering around the markets about what you are about to do. Besides, no serious capital will ever move before you publish your business plan, and that is at least 90 days away. This element is where you are inspired to begin thinking about your capital sources. To raise the score here, one or more of your management team and board members will have come from the industry. They are likely to know who does the investing, so ask them now and invite them to quietly explore the market for more answers.

Practical Experience—This Deserves the Minimum Weight of 1

Sometimes the capital is quite visible early in the life of the idea. An impressive idea backed by a strong management team is usually quick to be funded. You should expect to know the identity of the most promising source moments after your epiphany. The trick is to find a champion inside the funding source who will be smitten with your idea. Look for someone who has managed the funding of an enterprise in the industrial sector in which you expect to be active. I call this "smart money."Then, when the time is right you simply submit your business plan, keep your appointments to meet with him or her and push the process. And finally, a sobering thought: You will devote far more time to raising capital than you ever thought possible or necessary.

Dr. Market's Observation:

Beware the rats. There are financial preda-
tors out there who may attempt to convince
you that they can find your millions of dollars in seed or first-round financing. They
will sound and look great. Their price will be
control of your company or the CEO's chair or some other
highly elevated position. One thing will lead to another and
they will take over your company. Then they might pocket
all the available cash and squander the assets, often on preposterous contracts with their family or friends. How do
you spot them up front? You protect yourself by examining
their relationships and ties to responsible bankers and other
resources. Only deal with people who are properly introduced to both you and the right investors. Also, do your
own due diligence on the people who will try to help you
find your first money. Never let an incongruity go unsolved.

Examples

Assuming you have in mind a management team that will attract
capital, you should now be identifying the angels, seed investors,
and possibly the companies who really need for you to succeed.
Venture capitalists? Take their business cards and initiate a serious
relationship but don't ask for money or submit any business plans
until after you have obliterated your risks and demonstrated
significant market appeal of your products. If you are lucky, you
will never need to work with them. Often, however, they will be
your only salvation. When the time is right for venture capital, the
relationship building you do today will become quite valuable.

The Coin-Operated Laundry—
Visible Capital score: 9

Fortunately, this business requires only a modest amount of capital. You are leasing property and probably leasing the equipment, and using other people's resources. The capital requirements are modest and the capital should be visible because frankly they are so modest. The score for this enterprise at this early moment should be about a 9.

Element 35, Visible Capital *score summary:*
Weight 1 x Score 9 = Total 9

HARVEST

Introduction

Now that you have realized you have an idea worthy of consideration, you will need to consider the harvest. How big could this become? How valuable could it be? When could you convert the value to cash or some other form of financial advantage? These things should be considered at an early moment, and this is the section where they are raised.

Element 36

HIGH POTENTIAL VALUE

Value is the life-giving power of anything; cost, the quantity of labour required to produce it; its price, the quantity of labour which its possessor will take in exchange for it.
— John Ruskin, British art critic and author.
Munera Pulveris, ch. 1, 1872.

Definition

High Potential Value is the estimated value of the enterprise after about year five. The upper end can be anywhere within modesty and the low end should probably be something in excess of $100 million. At this tender stage of the process, a reasonable estimate is about three times the revenues or 10 or more times the earnings of year five. It should not be difficult to imagine a venture that reaches such altitudes after year five, unless of course it is a dot-com (where the time was routinely extended to 15 years).

Relevance—Why Add This Element?

Its long-term potential could be the most important reason why resources, management, board members, and prospective vendors will be attracted to your enterprise. The higher the potential, the less likely there will be excruciating due diligence up front—people become mesmerized by the possibilities.

High Potential Value is intended to smoke out those opportunities that are certain to attract attention while sidestepping those that are not. If there is high potential value, then a certain magnetic aura begins to emerge, it is a glow that causes the geniuses with insider knowledge to imagine the possibilities. These possibilities include particularly the cornucopia of valuable relationships that could result from even a modest success. Supporters such as law firms and other resources begin to consider your venture as something of an annuity where flows of related or unrelated clientele flow as a result of their affiliation with your venture. Quite often the magnetism of the idea will result in unsolicited offers of support from enthusiastic prospective vendors. It can also attract attention that invites competition (there are legal tactics available for minimizing the potential of premature competition, not the least of which is allowing the public to witness the idea or venture only after appropriate protection). This then is one of the important lights in the sky that will attract attention of investors, management, board candidates, and other resources that you are seeking. Is it possible for this venture to become genuinely valuable?

Where to Find This Answer

To be absolutely certain of long-range potential you need to have completed your business plan. There are however clues in the industry such as comparable sales prices or price/earnings ratios of publicly traded companies with similar products. Remember, you are not buttoning down a number here and you are not writing your business plan. You are estimating a potential value that could apply to your enterprise five years from now.

Score Elevation Tactics

The moment an idea comes to mind, the question of value looms. A problem often unfolds when the answer is unrealistically high. The key here is assessing the certainty that the idea will be able to turn into more than $100 million in value. If it is absolutely certain to achieve such a level, stop. Do not, at this early stage, attempt to divine a value higher than high. Let the experts toy with that number in their own minds.[1]

Now then, what if the item scores too low? How can weight be added to the idea? There are a variety of strategies, any one of which could improve the score. Let's examine a few:

1. Logical maximum scale—Is it possible to portray the maximum extent the enterprise can reach? Where do the costs begin to erode as you attempt to manage a far-flung enterprise? Where do the revenue forecasts dip below any rational minimum necessary to sustain an operating unit?

2. Duplication—Is it possible to duplicate your concept into another country?

---

1. It is at this point that I often write a capital B in the top-right corner of the blackboard. My students and I have a quiet chat about never uttering the word "billion" but never miss an opportunity to feed the optimist with facts and figures that any reasonable person would conclude is further assurance that you are aiming far too low in valuation. Let the listener's brains do the math. These are the people who attended the great business schools and who are far smarter than anyone else in these matters. Feed them but don't gag them.

3. Franchising—Are the financial dynamics well suited for franchising?

4. Roll up—Is it possible to acquire other enterprises doing similar things in remote locations? Where do the costs, revenues, and market dynamics circumscribe the limits to any rational roll up strategy? What are the harvest implications?

5. Strategic partnering—Actually, we covered this in Element 29. Does the value chain in this business offer any candidates for strategic partnering? Can a partnership avoid the potential of your being devoured at a price below your full harvest potential?

6. Licensing—Can any aspect of the venture be patented or licensed to others for the fullest market realization?

Practical Experience—This Deserves the Maximum Weight of 3

There has never been anything as enchanting in new venture launching as the possibility that the venture could reach an astronomical value. Even today as the dot-com bubble bursts and the rubble begins to accumulate at our feet, the prospect of high value is still the most likely reason why people become excited about new ventures. Yes, lemons still bloom in two years and plums bloom in seven or more. But the possibility that your venture will soar into the atmosphere is still the most energizing thing that can happen.

Examples

Hindsight always has perfect vision and today we can observe that those courageous souls who backed Microsoft, Cisco, Sun, Apple,

Echostar, Southwest Air, and the various startups in wireless that have long since been rolled up foresaw the high potential value of their investment. The real achievement is being able to articulate your vision long before the only view in sight is hindsight. How can you explain that this idea will soar in value without looking silly?

Many businesses that might be worthy of pursuit are of modest potential. They can be lifestyle ventures or businesses that are not so much entrepreneurial as they are jobs working for one or several customers. There would be little potential for growth and the resources might be overwhelmed by scale. In the end, however, if your idea is genuinely worthy, it will not be preposterous to catch sight of a valuation potential in the range of one billion dollars. Stop and think about the numbers for a second. This situation could exist if it is possible to foresee somewhere in the future an enterprise with $70 million in revenues, a net margin of 15%, and a PE of 100 (suggesting that the investing public adored your business).[2] Clearly, that is not asking the impossible—most high-technology firms enjoyed these parameters throughout the 1990s, and even today PEs in excess of 100 are not rare. This is being done today, even after the dot-com bubble burst.

The Coin-Operated Laundry— High Potential Value score: 2

It appears that this is definitely not a high potential value business. You're running a Coin-Operated Laundry and a cleaners. It is possible that your cash flows will be strong but your High Potential Value will not. It deserves a 2, maximum. Or does it? How can you improve this score? Build more locations, roll up competitors who become available, acquire other companies, arrange for exclusivity

---

2. Simply calculated, a 15% margin on $70 million in revenues derives an earnings figure of $10,500,000. A public market PE of 100 suggests a valuation of $1,050,000,000. Bingo.

throughout your market, press for an exclusive franchise, push for excellence, preempt whenever you can, dominate the market. These are all tactics that are whispered to you throughout the Scorecard. You should be able to elevate this score immediately.

> ## Element 36, High Potential Value *score summary:*
> Weight 3 x Score 2 = Total 6

Element 37

FORESEEABLE HARVEST

Come, ye thankful people, come, Raise the song of harvest-home;
All is safely gathered in, Ere the winter storms begin.
—Henry Alford, "Come, Ye Thankful People, Come," 1844.

Definition

Foreseeable Harvest asks how the investor can expect to retrieve his or her investment. Can you predict that you will undertake an IPO? When? Or, will the company simply hang on and provide the owners with an enormous cash flow each month? Could the company be sold? Who might acquire it? Can the investor see both where his money is going and when and how much is coming back? Not to worry if there is more than one way to harvest.

Relevance—Why Add This Element?

Understanding this element could have a significant impact upon how attractive investors think your enterprise is. It is the harvest portrait that could sufficiently reassure an investor to actually make the commitment. Can you "see" the harvest and position the venture to greatest advantage?

Dr. Market's Observation:
Take care in soliciting funds at this stage—because of the laws surrounding solicitation of funds (the so-called Blue Sky Laws), it is never too early to enlist the advice of a lawyer who is knowledgeable in raising money.

Where to Find This Answer

You may not be able to predict the harvest precisely, but you should make a guess. Can it be predicted that a future cash flow stream will be robust and growing? Perhaps an IPO could be expected. What if a steady cash stream could be established and sustained without noteworthy growth? Perhaps a build-and-hold strategy could work best.

Score Elevation Tactics

Confidence and certainty of harvest direction, coupled with a rational justification, will elevate this score—prevaricate and you are doomed. Explain in a firm voice that you intend to harvest by maintaining hold on a cash cow, selling to a big company, or selling stock through an IPO. When in doubt, an enthusiastic prediction of an IPO should be safe because that is exactly where the venture capital firm will take you. You may also consider fixing the rights today for a registration sometime in the future. However, that might make it difficult for you to raise another round later because it limits the flexibility of the venture capital firm to create a workable deal.

Practical Experience—This Deserves the Minimum Weight of 1

This is a critical underlying question that drives all investors—when do I see my money come back? The typical harvest expectation is IPO and some of the more aggressive investors will seek registration rights to assure themselves that a timely IPO will be on its way. However, with a number of ventures, the harvest came with the sale of the company to another company better suited to fund and manage the growth. The lesson is that when you can only foresee modest potential, try to sell. When you can foresee a strong potential, steer toward the IPO harvest and maintain control as long as possible.

Examples

Here are some of your choices, none of which are bad. Remember that all choices can culminate in the sale of the company. It's just a matter of how easy it will be to own and stay on top of the cash flows and share them with others.

1. Cash flow, hopefully comparable to a regional rain pipe during a torrential downpour that you have somehow succeeded in anchoring above your head.

2. Asset sales, piece by piece, until you have an enterprise that provides you with ample cash flows and few if any shareholders other than yourself. This would be akin to buying a large

parcel of land, carving off and selling that portion that would be necessary to pay for the whole purchase, and living on the remaining parcel.

3. Partnering whereby you attach your company to a large enterprise.

4. IPO where you register your stock with the NASD and sell it to the public at large. This is where your investors are likely to push you, possibly through terms in your investment agreements (be aware of registration rights), unless you have a great explanation about the virtues of other alternatives.

5. Merger with or acquisition by someone else—they can be smaller or larger, just so the check clears the bank.

The Coin-Operated Laundry— Foreseeable Harvest score: 9

This is a matter that is somewhat peculiar or unique to the entrepreneur and the opportunity. Let's assume that you foresee a build and hold high cash flow strategy. If that can be projected at this time, say so. It would therefore score an 8 or 9. Let's call it a 9. If you were to score low, how would you build the number? It could depend upon how long it will take before you initiate any serious cash flow. It could also depend upon the tax treatment for your industry and the amount of outside capital required to launch (outside capital will almost certainly indicate that you will be going public soon).

> Element 37, Foreseeable Harvest *score summary:*
> Weight 1 x Score 9 = Total 9

DAUNTING
NEGATIVES

Introduction

This is the doomsday section where you must weigh where you could go terribly wrong. One of the items is an invitation to press on and overcome. The other two are more sinister in their potential impact. It is sometimes easier to overcome a big and brassy showstopper than it is to conquer something about which you are pretending not to know.

Element 38

TABOO

A sacred prohibition put upon certain people, things, or acts
which makes them untouchable or unmentionable.
Also any social prohibition or restriction that
results from convention or tradition.
—*Webster's New Universal Unabridged Dictionary at page 1855.*

Definition

Taboos are products that violate some societal or cultural norm and that will trigger a sharp, antagonistic reaction by your market against you or your products.

Relevance—Why Add This Element?

How receptive is the consuming public to your product? Score low and watch your ability to win customers dwindle. Watch too for

249

activist groups that could organize and mobilize boycotts against your product or your company. Anticipate and overcome these problems early by neutralizing the offensive features, possibly through the use of a countervailing publicity campaign.

Where to Find This Answer

Look for political correctness. Be sensitive to names and history, particularly when race is involved. Beware of health issues, ex-convicts in management, relationships with the FBI, zealous practice of religion, public nudity, promotion of the use of handguns, and promotion of smoking. Try to avoid things that make lots of noise (sorry, Harley-Davidson), glorify the consumption of alcohol, or promote gambling. On the international front, be careful with old adversaries such as France and Germany, Ireland and England, Pakistan and India, Israel and Islam, Poland and Russia,[1] and so on. This can be particularly true

Dr. Market's Observation:

 Beware the impact of crossing a border. You must visit with your agent or agents in the foreign country and clear the names and other working terminology of your firm. Favorite examples include the Korean "KIA" automobile sold in the United States. For tens of millions of military veterans, the one thing that leaps to mind is "Killed In Action," the phrase used when you die fighting.

---

1. One of my favorite experiences in this regard came in Siberia. We were discussing taboos in potential relationships with Germans and I was surprised to hear a unanimous chorus of "no's." Not one of the 25 members of the class had any reservations about dealing with the Germans. "Why," I asked? "Because we kicked their...[use your imagination]." There followed uproarious laughter.

when you introduce a third nation or flag in a bilateral negotiation. At home, taboos can be present in Native American matters, African American matters, and regional differences such as between the Northeast and Texas. In the end we can only hope that a taboo is more suspected than real, but you should be careful.

Score Elevation Tactics

Most taboos can be avoided with the application of simple intellectual horsepower. Do your homework if you are entering sensitive territory. You can also neutralize the taboo with preemptive public relations that spin the story in your favor early in the game. Perhaps the market for those who view the topic as attractive is big enough to sustain the business. Examples of taboos overcome include Playboy, tobacco, firearms, alcohol, Middle-Eastern food products, and gambling casinos.

Practical Experience—This Deserves the Medium Weight of 2

Taboos are hard to overcome. They often extend deep into the psyche of the consuming public and it is probably not a good idea to attempt to overcome them with your will and the investor's money. While it certainly could be possible to overcome many taboos with a PR campaign, my experience is that many of these problems are just too big to tackle for a new little company. Sometimes Mrs. Reagan had the right answer: "Just say no."[2] Today, now, when nothing has been cast into stone, make the adjustment to avoid any taboos.

---

2. This was the first lady's campaign slogan to rid schools of drugs.

Examples

Here are some wicked taboos, among many, that should be avoided:

1. Using the names of the deceased, assuming you could clear the intellectual property rights owned by the heirs.

2. Unflattering acronyms. In the 1950s the village of Indian Hill created its school system and gave serious thought to honoring its most famous resident who lived just down the street from the school. His name was Robert A. Taft.

3. Nudity—the 220-volt open line in society today. We love it but when we get too close to it we become electrocuted with near-universal condemnation.

4. Military-themed channels on cable television. Like nudity, it is alluring stuff but good luck in raising $100 million and attracting distribution commitments from the top six cable system owners.

5. Health matters, religion, race, personal physical dimensions, weight, or true hair color, although age and height seem to suffer well in public view.

The Coin-Operated Laundry—
Taboo score: 10

Clean clothes are hardly the stuff of taboos. Unless you name your venture N. Olympia in a Hispanic section of town[3] your venture should remain exempt from taboo issues. I would score this a 10. If this element were to score low for whatever reason, the logical response would be to remove the irritant either directly or indirectly. Check the name, check the advertising and promotion copy, check the neighborhood, and move forward with great respect for the people that will be your customer base—all of them.

> Element 38, Taboo *score summary:*
> Weight 2 x Score 10 = Total 20

---

3. No limpia, phonetically similar, means "no clean" in Spanish. If you are on North Olympia Street, you might want to avoid using the street address for the name.

Element 39

LACK OF
SHOWSTOPPERS

*Mankind is composed of two sorts of men—those who love and
create, and those who hate and destroy.*
—Jose Marti, letter to a Cuban farmer, 1893.

Definition

Showstoppers can be devastating, terminating barriers to success.
If you proceed with your idea, is there certain to be a forceful push-
back that stops your venture?[1] Will the public announcement of
your existence result in your being obliterated by a competitor, a
legal barrier, another country, or worst of all, someone who does not

---

1. The term is twisted from the normal definition, which is a positive. A showstopper
is defined as a theatrical performance or person that is so robust, so beautiful, so
arresting that it literally "stops the show." Here I use the term in its business context: Is there something that will stop your show such that it dies or is stillborn?

255

trust the legal system for adequate redress against you (such that they take the law into their own hands)? Note the polarity on this score. The more you *lack* showstoppers, the higher you score.

Dr. Market's Observation:

If this score is a zero or below, there is likely to be extraordinary value if you can overcome the showstopper. The reason is that if you can overcome it, you might accomplish something in which others have tried and failed. The message of an appallingly low score just could be—persist.

Relevance—Why Add This Element?

A showstopper is some aspect of the game that will simply stop you dead. It is obviously relevant because it can preempt your ability to succeed. It is not an element easy to overcome. However, if it is recognized up front, there might be a way to eliminate it. Quite often the showstoppers are simply ephemeral images, much like the Wizard of Oz.[2]

Where to Find This Answer

The range of possibilities here is extensive. First of all, the odds are quite high that you deserve a 10 here. However if there *is* such a thing confronting you, score your idea below a 5. If the showstopper has some genuine penalties such as financial or physical, consider a negative score depending upon the penalty.

---

2. In case you don't remember, the Wizard was a guy behind the drapes pulling levers and pushing buttons that made it all appear real, when it was all an elaborate hoax.

Showstoppers are often legal in nature. Look for laws, treaties, or administrative policies in government agencies that could prevent you from accomplishing your objective. There are also significant possibilities relating to access to distribution and critical suppliers. Note also the potential difficulties created by user groups or other customer alliances that favor your competition. This is what it feels like when someone has inspired their legislator to insert some protective language into a statute. They create a showstopper for people like you.

Dr. Market's Observation:

 Few showstoppers are weaker than barriers that appear to be legal in nature. Please don't take the lawyering into your own hands. Have a pro help you get around the showstopper legally. The U S Constitution addresses something called "due process" and that means there is normally always a way to change the law. The point? If there is a realistic way to change the law without spending a lot of money, and if the rewards are overwhelming, factor the delays into your thinking and proceed quickly before someone learns what you know about removing the barrier.

Score Elevation Tactics

If you can circumvent the showstopper, you are often on the path to success because no one else would have the courage to challenge it.

If the showstopper is somehow vulnerable, it is almost certain to be accompanied by an attitude of hubris by the beneficiaries. If you are about to overcome the showstopper, do so in absolute and strictest confidentiality. This will allow for an increase in your score. Sometimes a showstopper can be vulnerable to a political maneuver. Can you insert some political protection against a response by the owner of the showstopper? Can you create the image of a preemptive barrier to a showstopper response? Can you create a legal barrier, such as the threat of antitrust, breach of contract violation of some intellectual property right, patent infringement, or other litigation?

Customer alliances, particularly in situations where the owner of the showstopper is not popular, can be effective. However, they take time and you can lose the element of surprise if the campaign is extended. If the industry suffers from limited suppliers or distributors, it might be possible to obliterate the showstopper with a counter move that creates a competitor, perhaps several.

Practical Experience—This Deserves the Maximum Weight of 3

Showstoppers are perceived to be very real problems but they are often apocryphal, as in of doubtful authenticity, false, fictitious, or spurious. Never be daunted by these showstoppers until you have tried everything and even then sometimes you can get lucky. Conventional wisdom on these matters must be tested. However, in the end, if the showstopper *cannot* be removed, your show is over.

Examples

Here are some possibilities:

1. A law—statute, regulation, judicial interpretation, or treaty from a municipality, county, state, or federal government that has an economic or trade-protective essence.

2. Your critical set of customers are in a dwindling industry—you cannot succeed if your customer base is evaporating.

3. Internet disintermediation when you are trying to be an intermediary.

The Coin-Operated Laundry—Lack of Showstoppers score: 7

Can you foresee a monumental problem? Will your chemicals be outlawed someday? Is your plant soon to be branded as a toxic waste dump? It is possible for a little cleaning and Coin-Operated Laundry business to encounter a showstopper. However, it's not likely. Let's score it a 7 because of the potential for some trouble, but not much. Elevating a bad score here means specifying the threat and then neutralizing it. Change the chemicals. Clean up the toxic waste. Make the premises look like a surgical suite, with great attention to cleanliness and lack of refuse.

> Element 39, Lack of Showstoppers *score summary:*
> Weight 3 x Score 7 = Total 21

Element 40

PRETENDING NOT TO KNOW

The easiest thing of all is to deceive one's self, for what a man wishes he generally believes to be true.
—Demosthenes

Definition

Pretending Not to Know could be the most bizarre of the elements, compliments of David Carl Gwinn, the fellow who explained it to me after having heard it at a dinner party in Los Angeles. What is the entrepreneur pretending not to know that could be critical? More often than not, the answer is "nothing." In that case enter a max score of 10 and move forward. However, there are moments when this question smokes out a severe and sometimes insurmountable problem.

Perhaps another way of describing this problem is myopia. Causes can vary from greed, enthusiasm for success, hyperconfidence, some misguided impression or misunderstanding, and dare-devilishness, to some other cause that obstructs cool, sound reasoning. Whatever the cause, the result is that the investor finds an entrepreneur who is pretending not to know that he or she is in trouble with the idea, who is blind to the problem and insists upon not seeing or understanding it.

Relevance—Why Add This Element?

There are a number of reasons why this element is quite important. For example:

1. It means you insist upon not seeing something that is obvious to the investor.

2. It means that you do not listen, see, or hear critical information.

3. It means that you cannot assimilate critical information and reason.

4. It means that you may not understand your business.

5. It means that you are inflexible.

Where to Find This Answer

Common sense is often the arbiter on this element. Any investor or investment advisor with a modicum of seasoning will have the required vision to see and react to an entrepeneur's myopia. It is not difficult to sense blind spots. Unfortunately it is also not difficult to see a blind spot in someone else when it does not exist. This means that you should be careful in drawing conclusions—

people can always surprise you, particularly when you are betting that they are being stupid.

Dr. Market's Observation:

We have today one of the most remarkable tools ever devised for protection against business myopia—the Internet. Never fail to use search tools such as *www.google.com*, *www.ask.com*, or *www.refdesk.com* when you suspect you are misinformed or naïve about the market you are contemplating. Watch attentively for signs of competition.

Score Elevation Tactics

Quietly check the idea—ask some trusted people if you are ignoring something obvious. Call your resource candidates and call your distribution candidates. Twist the facts slightly to protect your idea and your venture (remember, you really have no protection just now) and ask them to describe the competition. Validate your venture and your products.

Practical Experience—This Deserves the Minimum Weight of 1

It is surprising how many times this question scores low. Entrepreneurs pretend not to know that there is competition, that there is no demand, that there is a law against what they contemplate, that you cannot guarantee any exclusivity, or even that your idea is simply in poor taste.

Dr. Market's Observation:

More often than not, you can overcome the problem easily if you can see past your blind spot. When you insist on ignoring it, it takes a life of its own and overwhelms your chances of success.

Examples

Here are some possible ways that people pretend not to know something important:

1. Probably the most common example is a refusal to believe that there are competitors vigorously seining these waters, collecting all your customers in their nets. You may be defining the market too narrowly and pretending not to know that there is a vigorous competitor or two. Ready substitutes are available that offer the key features and benefits. Worse, these substitutes could be offered at aggressive prices with long-term contracts that preempt and ensure domination of the market by your competitors.

2. An enterprise that can only be a nonprofit organization that is pretending to be a for-profit organization.

3. Creating a business for sending video via cell phones pretending not to know that the wireless network is not yet capable of managing that kind of traffic. It could be a while before the network has that capability.

4. Unless you have an ironclad, sustainable uniqueness such as with a patent, another type of pretend is the refusal to acknowledge an obvious ambush. Whatever *un*sustainable

uniqueness you may possess will be obliterated by a bigger, better-established, and better-funded potential perpetrator of an ambush. For those who believe that a new PC operating system would overwhelm the market because of its magnificence, the pretend is that Microsoft would do nothing to thwart it.

5. Another problem can involve the mistaken belief that a market exists when it does not. Cues include an inability to identify any customer who would buy the products. One example involved a group from Tennessee that in 2001 was attempting to market the intellectual DNA of the architectural drawings of a famous and now-deceased architect. They had a wonderful vision and they were quite passionate about it. However, there was no product evident for which demand could have been created. There was no business, and they were pretending not to know it.

6. The entrepreneur may not comprehend the dimensions of the integrity and honesty problems. This is a significant issue that is difficult to perceive, and once understood, even more difficult to manage. However, as we have learned from the travails of a great number of sports figures and celebrities, the half-life of a bad image is but a few years, if that.

7. Sometimes the entrepreneur simply fails to convey the business concept or the uniqueness in a way that is comprehensible by the average investor. He or she may simply not understand it well enough to explain it. I was once involved in just such a case; the scientist was certain she could deliver a new way to multiply bandwidth in a fiber optic line, but she was unable to explain it, and with that the business collapsed. She was pretending not to know that no one could understand what she was saying.

The Coin-Operated Laundry—Pretending Not to Know score: 6

Are you pretending not to know something that is critically important? Are you in denial that the economy in your town is in a serious downturn with plant closings, massive layoffs, and a broad exodus? Are you pretending not to know that people just do not dress up in your town and that a cleaners is almost certain to fail? Are you pretending not to know that the new Wal-Mart nearby offers everything you are offering at a fraction of the price, and that no one in your town has clothes good enough to care about the difference in quality you hope to offer? Let's score this a 6 until we know more. Elevating this score could involve an escalation of service such that the Wal-Mart and others cannot compete. Alert the vendors of fine fabrics and garments to advise their customers that no stain is permanent in this town with the new cleaning services that you offer. Be realistic about your circumstances and be aggressive about correcting any myopia you might have about your community and this business opportunity.

> Element 40, Pretending Not to Know *score summary:*
> Weight 1 x Score 6 = Total 6

THE STORY

Introduction

This is the very first element to be honored in the life of a new venture. You weave and then tell the story to someone. You attempt to inspire support, attract resources, and win funding with a story that is both compelling and inspiring. This is where the parade from your mind to the market begins and it is one area that deserves constant attention as factors, features, and benefits change. Why is this topic offered so late in this book? Because the other elements are of higher priority and now, just now, you are finally able to consider the whole story.

Element 41

HIGH PROFILE PERSONS AVAILABLE

Fame sometimes hath created something of nothing.
—Thomas Fuller, *The Holy State and the Profane State*, 1642.

Definition

The involvement of a famous person, particularly one whose reputation was made in or near your market, can be a helpful plus at the early moments of a venture's existence. It is a speed catalyst. Listeners often have no other point of reference for credibility, legitimacy, or integrity. This element involves adding people onto the boards or management team who own a big name in the industry, politics, media, sports, or any other prominent place. These are people the customers and suppliers all know well. They have been in the news often. Anyone who possesses significant public recognition and access to other high-profile persons would qualify. *Ideally, however, they would be people who bring with them a coterie of friends from the industry in question.*

Relevance—Why Add This Element?

Why add this element? Because it is an astounding plus, a rocket blast, a 2,000-pound bomb explosion, an attention grabber like nothing else you will ever see within the first few days of your existence. Since you have no product and no company of which to speak, what can attract the attention of your resources as you attempt to win them over? Obviously the best way to attract their attention is the pure compelling force of your idea. However, since the average venture firm receives hundreds of proposals per week, you could use a simple one-liner that grabs attention. Why go through a lengthy description of your venture when you can simply say that "Bill Gates or Warren Buffett or Henry Kissinger or Diane Sawyer or Sally Ride or Madeleine Albright is a shareholder and member of the board." They are easy to recognize and the listener has no difficulty acknowledging that if these people were involved, surely the venture must be legitimate. The names build confidence and establish instant credibility at a time when they may be the only aspects of the venture that do. Note that the closer their connection to your product or your industry, the easier will be the connect. The justification for this borrowing of fame is the implication that if the listener were to accept the invitation, they too could enjoy a relationship with the star. It opens doors and moves you far more quickly toward your goal. During the first moments of the existence of your venture, these high-profile persons may be all you have to shore up confidence and credibility.

Where to Find This Answer

If your cause is not troubled by some public relations issue, and if you have access to the famous person through friends or family, make contact and attempt to win them over. Investors, resources, customers, and all manner of good can come from these relationships.

Dr. Market's Observation:

One sure sign of strength in your proposal will be the ready willingness of the really savvy high-profile persons to work with you, allowing you to use their name without up-front compensation. The truly sophisticated high-profile person realizes that they will be blessed many times over, including with the ability to invest when the stock is cheap. They will be quick to see the opportunity to "chat up" your venture in circles where you may never fly.

Score Elevation Tactics

The score for using high-profile persons could be among the easiest to elevate. Someday you can converse about the value of actually selling your product or service, but for now the most important thing is gaining credibility, and fast. Cast a wide net, and keep fishing until you have a big name or two. Note that your compensation for these people might vary, and could be high. One former secretary of state commands a high cash and/or equity compensation for using his name—five percent of equity, but only for the right opportunity. Keep reminding your celebrity that the real value will come later, when this enterprise is up and operational. Consulting contracts, board membership fees, options, and cheap stock are all possible. Weave your story well, allow for reasonable negotiation, sign your deal, and keep moving forward. Sources of high-profile individuals include a well-regarded law firm, friends and family, and your bank. Note also that this could be one of the very few aspects of an association with an accounting firm that could be of value at this early stage—they may have access to a star or two.

Practical Experience—This Deserves the Medium Weight of 2

The culture of one's upbringing can often influence how quickly the entrepreneur endorses the idea of using someone famous to help build quick confidence in your venture. In the rural areas of the Midwestern United States, this may not sit well. People there often eschew fame.[1] However, in urban areas of the country *including* the Midwest, it often strikes a sympathetic chord. Famous people can be lightning rods of attention, and oddly, an image of freedom from risk (despite the fact that their presence has little to do with reducing risk). There is also the possibility that investor or resource prospects will wish to be associated with winners, including just being associated with an enterprise that boasts of the famous participants you mention. It is part of the buzz you need to create.

---

1. The official medallion of Miami University, the old one in Ohio that was the source of the *McGuffey Reader* (the first attempt to promote long-distance learning away from the classroom) and the Cradle of Coaches, has a Latin inscription, front and center, that says "Prodesse Quam Conspici." You can look it up because it is still there. It means "Achievement without fame." Many alums have become quite shamelessly famous, suggesting that few took Latin or paused long enough to know that they should not be so noteworthy in their accomplishments. My apologies Miami, dear alma mater, but I could not resist. The point is that in the Midwest, this business about achievement without fame was once taken seriously.

It is consoling in many respects, and now, long before products are being delivered, at least you have these names "working" for you.

The value of using a high-profile person in your venture can be a perishable commodity—someday soon after launch, the reputation of the company and your products should trump the value of the name belonging to the high-profile person. In the end however the high-profile person energizes the team and the process, particularly if they take an active role.

While I am a believer in this element, there has always appeared to be an inverse relationship between the scale of the name and the amount of work they will deliver to your enterprise to make it succeed. Use the name up front to gain traction but as quickly as possible move beyond the time when it is valuable.

Examples

Possibilities of high-profile individuals—also known in the legal world as public figures—who could accelerate the advancement of your story include:

1. Any former high-profile CEO who did not leave under a cloud.

2. Film star with good image.

3. Sports figure with good image.

4. Political figure with good image.

The Coin-Operated Laundry—High-Profile Persons Available score: 7

Who are the top five people in your community, ranked by fame, who might allow their name and photograph to be involved with your company or its services? Remove the people from the list who would absolutely, positively not want to participate. Who would allow you to move forward? Remember that the profile needs to be from the midst of your customer base. If you are in a Hispanic neighborhood, it would be a good idea to find someone your clientele admires. Let's assign this a 7. How can we raise the score? Pick up the phone and win over the commitment of a person with a household name that is broadly recognized in your community. What about a local TV news anchor? They can be recently retired, and they can therefore come out of a political office. Think in terms of the outdoor advertisers' five-word maximum and consider a slogan that would emphasize the presence or support of your key high-profile person. "Cleanliness is next to Godliness" could be associated with one or several priests, ministers, nuns, rabbis, or imams. Sports figures, and stars of stage and screen might work best because they are so attentive to how they appear.

Element 41, High-Profile Persons Available
score summary:
Weight 2 x Score 7 = Total 14

Element 42

PUNCHY, COMPELLING STORY

Apathy can only be overcome by enthusiasm and enthusiasm can only be aroused by two things: first, an ideal which takes the imagination by storm, and second, a definite intelligible plan for carrying that ideal into practice.
—Arnold Toynbee

Definition

Using a punchy, compelling story sums up your most urgent need as you begin to attempt to convert your idea to value. Can you weave a story that is punchy and compelling? Can you touch on a few features and few benefits? Will the story prompt immediate action by the listener? Can it be short and gut wrenching? Is it something that would survive well the old telephone game where it travels from one talker to another?

Relevance—Why Add This Element?

The scoring of the punchy, compelling nature of your story is here because your idea is doomed to mediocrity or worse without it. It is your "elevator speech." Pretend you have just gotten in an elevator with the key decision maker of the firm you would like most to support you. You have 20 floors in which to respond to the following question: "So, what does your company do?" The ready-made punchy, compelling story is calculated to inspire action, if not by the listener then by his or her listener when they pass the story along. This is your primary sales and marketing tool for the earliest moments of your enterprise. Nothing else is available; no website, no brochure, no office, and possibly not even a business card.

Dr. Market's Observation:

 Note the ability of this story to carry itself through the variety of iterations necessary to reach the appropriate listeners. You will rarely be in front of the key people who need to hear your message—it will be told second- and third-hand. So keep it simple, punchy, and compelling. Your "sale" is likely to occur when the story is told far away from you.

Where to Find This Answer

Actually, weaving a punchy, compelling story should not be difficult. Place in front of yourself the features and benefits of your product. Make those changes that would be helpful. Then try to create a story that is both punchy and compelling. Will it save lives, cure diseases, make babies smart, guarantee a championship, abolish some key strategic costs, accelerate your customer's profits, restore youth and beauty or make the customer rich and famous?

Score Elevation Tactics

Improving the score means editing the story over and over again. Keep at it and remember that the shorter, punchier, and more compelling, the better. "I have here the cure for cancer in humans." That is a punchy, compelling story. Try to make the story so memorable that people will feel compelled or inspired to pass it along. The advertising industry—particularly outdoor advertising with its emphasis upon five words or less—is quite gifted at this game.

Practical Experience—This Deserves the Maximum Weight of 3

Like a great sauce, punchy, compelling stories require constant cooking, seasoning, and stirring to boil down to a wonderful essence that seizes the listener's attention the moment it is heard. Sometimes a little bit of shock value is helpful, such as "this software prevents the possibility of thieves stealing your identity and defrauding you and the FICO scoring system for your credit." Sometimes it is helpful to create a company slogan. "We will create a company that handles e-commerce returns and converts broken goods into customer satisfaction." "We will create a company that generates electricity from the natural gas that is vented and burned off of the Russian oilfields." "We will design, build, install, and operate the first undersea fiber optic cable that connects all the countries located on the Baltic Ocean." "We will create an airline that interconnects all commercial airfields located on Native American reservations in the United States, Canada, and Mexico." "We will establish the first Internet service provider in Turkey and sell computers that have its software pre-installed."

One more thought: try to avoid the use of hyperbole and modifiers. Do not use "fantastic," "home run," "colossal," and the like. You will only hurt yourself in front of the savvy listeners.

Examples

Here are some punchy and compelling statements:

1. This product cures cancer. Period.

2. When added to water and some newspapers this product creates the perfect insulation and barrier to heat and ballistic projectiles.

3. This product makes rubber vehicular tires impervious to wear.

4. This device, the size of a dime, when implanted in your brain will allow you to communicate by thought rather than by action.

The Coin-Operated Laundry—Punchy, Compelling Story score: 7

Your story for this business is not yet a best seller. You will have a challenge crafting a punchy, compelling story that will advance you into a sure success. You are about to open a Coin-Operated Laundry and a cleaners. The advantage you enjoy is one that involves a marginal improvement in quality and nothing more.

Until you come up with something better, the optimum score is therefore only a 4. My logic in this score is that it has some interesting features (the innovation), but that it cannot meet even a halfway mark to a perfect 10. How can it be improved? Hammer at the uniquenesses. "Our shop can't be beaten by any stain." "We save all great clothes and fabrics from ruination by stain and we plan on a nationwide roll out." Come to think of it, let's raise that score right now to a 7.

> **Element 42, Punchy, Compelling Story** *score summary:*
> Weight 3 x Score 7 = Total 21

CARPE DIEM

Introduction

Time is always of the essence. Among the thousands of things there are to do all at once, two areas beg for attention. Move quickly in the government arena even if there is only a remote chance of regulatory oversight. Note that your antagonists will sometimes attempt to cause your business to be regulated—it provides them with another way to harm your chances to succeed. The second area will remind you of a land grab. You must run through the markets as fast as possible collecting resources, people, advisors, directors, executives, funding, vendor advantages, and if you can, all the great customers. This is where an abiding sense of urgency must imbue the whole team. You need to run through the market and reach your goals in a New York minute!!!

Carpe diem.

Element 43

GOVERNMENT RELEVANCE

You can only govern men by serving them.
The rule is without exception.
—Victor Cousins

Definition

Ours is a market-driven economy functioning inside a democracy. Your job is to find ways to attach your market-driven, economically valuable idea to democracy wherever and whenever it is possible. Trust that those who wish you harm are working hard to find their points of attachment in the democracy even if you are not. This is where the imperatives of running a successful business must trump your political philosophy about whether the government should have a role in what you do.

Dr. Market's Observation:

 Before you become embroiled with a politician, you absolutely must familiarize yourself with the laws involving campaign contributions. The money goes by check to their election campaign treasurer and there are strict limits on the amount you can contribute. You are also prohibited from handing them a check in certain places and even talking to them about a contribution from their office telephone! Be very careful here. Again, *your lawyer should know what you should do and you must talk to him or her about this before you do anything.*

Relevance—Why Add This Element?

Consider the wisdom of having a statute that makes it illegal to compete with you. Within certain well-defined bounds, this is exactly what happens. There are literally thousands of incredibly gifted people in Washington, the state capitals, and the cities and counties throughout America practicing an art of persuading legislators and politicians to protect their clients. We call them lobbyists, a term born in the 19th century when legislators met with them in the lobby of the Willard Hotel in Washington.

Working with politicians is sometimes a game of first come, first served, and you have to move quickly. Elected officials, including especially the congressional delegations in Washington, often have access to the tops of every key company or institution in America. Lobbying can also mean trouble with ambush and showstoppers as well as competitors—so do your homework before you approach these people (if you are fortunate, your biggest antagonist will be in another district governed by a member of the opposing political party[1]). There is enormous horsepower residing here. Be careful, but trust that new jobs, revenue streams, and potential new campaign contributors might be sufficiently attractive to the politician to prove valuable for you and your investors in winning their support. To be sure, you must beware of the fundraising realities of *their* lives but jobs and value creation are often so important to them that they will do what they can to ensure your success (with the unstated expectation that success will result in campaign contributions). Make certain that you understand and honor the political flags—note whether the politician is Democrat or Republican (don't think that this political flag business is not important). Finally, there are trade associations such as National Small Business United whose mission it is to lobby small business issues on your behalf nationwide. You should always be aware of their "hot button" issues of the day because those issues probably apply to you too.

Where to Find This Answer

Government Relevance is easy to manage quickly on the Internet. Simply look up the identities of the political people around you and understand their legislative committee assignments. If there is a connect—a way for you to communicate easily with a certain politician because his or her views and experiences are so similar—contact the legislator or his or her chief of staff to set up an appointment. Your objective should be to tell your story and relate it to legislative initiatives that could help or hinder your success. You should also know that your legislators are often exceptional match makers.

---

1. They have to be over there in the other district or else they are not likely to be very powerful. Right? They will not be able to take the floor and make the case for your position. This is why they call it political science.

Score Elevation Tactics

First of all, and quick because this is an up-front question, who is your governor, the mayor, and the congressional delegation? What are the committee assignments? What story will captivate their attention? The closer the match between your interests and theirs, the higher the score. If the score moves downward because of what you discover, consider a move to a more attractive district— sometimes there is development capital waiting for you to do so, such as across the bridge in the neighboring state.

Dr. Market's Observation:

If you can foresee a way for your local legislator or head of government to assist you, add points to the score here. If your total score warrants taking the next step, talk to your lawyer about the lobbying potential. He or she is guaranteed to know enough about the law-creating legislative process to be of assistance—they had to pass the bar exam and constitutional law is the Holy Grail for this activity. Your challenge will be to find something that protects your company without necessarily blessing your competition. This is tricky but doable.

Practical Experience—This Deserves the Medium Weight of 2

It is often quite valuable to find a mayor, governor, congressman, or senator to take up your story as a matter of political interest. You do not need to communicate directly with the elected officials but you should expect to be in contact with their staffs. This works for industries where there is likely to be government regulation and for many where regulation is a remote possibility. If you are near these areas, you can *always* find a politician to support you.

Furthermore, plan on establishing relationships with the congress immediately after your funding arrives. Without giving away secrets, let them know what you are doing. Befriend a senior staffer. Consider what you require from the congress. Replicate the efforts at the state level. This maneuver can be critical to your success because you could be joined soon by "me-too" competitors. Someone may be about to go to the president, the congress, or the state governments with demands to "level the playing field," which normally means a long uphill climb for you. This is suitable advice for nearly every industrial sector.

Note that if you are about to make a thunderous announcement and the congress, the administration, or any government agency will be affected, you absolutely, positively must stop by their offices immediately before you go public. No exceptions. Someday you will need these people so you should bring them into your family now.

Dr. Market's Observation:

 Politicians by definition have opponents. If you fail to win the endorsement of someone, then you must approach their legislative opponents and their political opponents. This could be the only place where you will gain traction in government circles so keep your options open, and try to not fly your own personal political flag. If you are a Republican, rest assured that someday your success will absolutely, positively depend upon a Democrat, and vice versa.

Examples

Examples here should be no mystery, but for the sake of completeness, here are some possibilities:

1. The mayor of your city can influence matters relating to your local activities including property, zoning, parking, and so on.

2. The chief political office holder(s) in your county can also influence matters relating to your local activities including property, zoning, parking, and so on.

3. The district attorney, state or federal, can be instrumental in defining how he or she will enforce a law that has a particularly acute bearing upon your business.

4. The county sheriff or chief of police can sometimes work with you regarding how he or she will enforce or manage the enforcement of laws within his or her purview, including traffic, traffic patterns, signs, and so on.

5. The governor or state legislators can make or amend state laws that have a bearing upon your business.

6. The administration in Washington (from the president through all the cabinet-level agencies) has enormous power, particularly in the areas covered by the cabinet secretaries. If you don't like what you see, and if you cannot prevail there, turn east and visit your congressman or senator.[2] Almost all the time they have a mirror image of legislative activity.

7. Congress can be very helpful where both the house and the senate deliberate upon statutory protections and exemptions that are inserted into the laws each and every day.

---

2. Capitol Hill is about 2 miles east southeast of the White House.

8. Quasi-independent agencies such as the FCC can be rich sources of political leverage that you should treat much as if they were cabinet agencies (the distinctions are too subtle for you to be concerned about).

9. Staff leaders in all levels of all government (federal, state, and local) are the people who manage and oversee the process much like the First Sergeants in an infantry platoon. They can often succeed in situations where you do not need to visit with their bosses (the politicians).

10. Leadership of the political parties can be extremely powerful because they often control the flow of cash and other political support necessary to ensure re-election.

11. Be aware that all the political counterparts to all the people that you have contacted on the list above are splendid back-ups for you—don't let the wrong election outcome terminate your business.

The Coin-Operated Laundry— Government Relevance score: 10

What possible corner of the federal, state, or local government would find you to be interesting? OSHA, EPA, and other safe guardians are always on the prowl for trouble. That is the sinister side of government relations. And the upside? Watch for opportunities to promote your products *politically* to museum curators; owners of uniforms for military, police, bands, sports teams, and the like; representatives of districts with large job counts in fine fabrics and suit/dress manufacturing, and so on. There is a solid relevance to your business.

Element 43, Government Relevance *score summary:*
Weight 2 x Score 10 = Total 20

Element 44

LOW HANGING FRUIT

The ripest fruit first falls.
—William Shakespeare, *King Richard the Second*,
act II, scene I, line 154, 1595.

Definition

Is there anything that is easy to attract, win, or (much like ripe fruit) pick? Are there any prospective customers who would pay a portion of the full price just to be able to lock up some of your initial production? Is there any candidate for any management position who is world class and looking for a job? Are there any vendors who would be enthusiastic about helping a company such as yours now? Are there any politicians poised to grasp for the promise of your products and who would do anything to make sure you thrived? Are there any distributors who would add the promise of your product today? Are there any investors brimming with cash who know your industry and would love to support you?

Relevance—Why Add This Element?

Speed is the primary driving motive in seeking low-hanging fruit. This is the land of the New York minute. How fast can the enterprise reach some level of irreversible momentum? How many critical issues can be solved or at least greatly alleviated by grabbing the fruit within easy reach? Can enough key issues be addressed to make a successful launch inevitable?

Where to Find This Answer

Begin by telling the story as quickly as you can to people in all critical aspects of your business. Get the word out to lawyers, bankers,

---

Dr. Market's Observation:

 Don't be surprised if exploiting these early low-hanging-fruit opportunities could have a dramatic influence on the strategic direction and scale of the enterprise. Don't fight it too hard by being stuck in your thinking about the strategic direction of your business. You are after all at the very front end of taking a thought to market—*everything* is subject to change. The author launched a satellite company and watched an underwater fiber optic cable to the same destination sail through the regulatory process without a scratch. Why? No one had ever thought to regulate it. He and his team knew the satellite business and by gosh they were going to launch one!

---

prospective managers and board members, and other helpers who may have quick access to other low-hanging fruit. Perhaps the most important role of all senior managers in the earliest moments of the idea's existence is to grab the low-hanging fruit in all directions.

Score Elevation Tactics

Time and incessant attention to this element will result in an improved score. It is one element that must be at the front of your thinking every day—how can you grab the next piece of low-hanging fruit? As senior advisors are attracted to the enterprise, they will all bring their own families of contacts and affiliations, each one bringing a tree with low-hanging fruit. Therefore the optimum score elevation tactic will be to converse with people who are in a position to deliver something important immediately.

Practical Experience—This Deserves the Modest Weight of 1

If you cannot pick off a basket full of "fruit" for your venture within a week of trying, stop for a moment and verify that you have a business on your hands. I have never seen a venture that has

Dr. Market's Observation:

You do not have to compromise your secrets in your quest for low-hanging fruit. Don't give people you are attempting to woo more information than is absolutely necessary to allow them to make a judgment to support you. They do not need to know your secrets right now.

a sustainable uniqueness serving a compelling unserved need that cannot accumulate a rich bounty of ripe fruit immediately, and long before the business plan is written.

Examples

Here is where I would look for low-hanging fruit:

1. Law firm (don't be surprised if you need to go out of town because of lack of skill or conflict of interest).

2. Executives of firms in your value chain.

3. Customers.

4. Resources (with exclusive deals?).

5. Distribution (with exclusive deals?).

6. Government support (particularly the city, state, and congressional delegations).

7. Board of directors.

8. Board of advisors.

9. Friends and family.

10. Friends of friends and family.

11. High-profile persons whose replacement has just been announced—suddenly they are free molecules.

12. Companies that are in Chapter 11. The trustee will be aggressive in helping you accumulate some extremely low-cost assets, including furniture, vehicles, and the like.

13. Highly talented people who have been let go or who are "on the beach." Location is probably irrelevant—they will chase your employment opportunity even if their first payday won't be for several months.

14. Companies or resources that have announced expansion into markets where you need to tap support—they could be just a bit hungry.

15. Alums of your schools, especially high school, college or university.

16. Board of trustees of your college or university.

17. Military connections: of course my favorite is the not-so-secret society known as "ex-Marines." SEALs, Rangers, Green Berets, Air Force Search andRescue, and the Coast Guard are also all spring-loaded to help you if you are an "alum."

The Coin-Operated Laundry— Low-Hanging Fruit score: 7

Looking out over the possible actions that can be concluded within the next two to four weeks, what is the value of these activities? Can you close a deal with a resource, a management team member, a board member, a famous person, a distributor, or best of all, a large business-saving customer? Can you lock up an unfair advantage that no one will know about for years but who will ensure the life and vitality of your business? Can you win over the allegiance, if not actually close with a funding resource? What percentage of the critical milestones of your business can be put to rest within the next two to four weeks? Let's assume you deserve a passing score here, a 7. How might you increase the score? I would recommend two directions. First, create your list of critical strategic milestones and ask yourself what can be conquered quickly given your personal circumstances. The other approach is from the other direction—what are all of your resources, contacts, and quick-position possibilities? Is there anyone out there who could use a sale to another user? Absolutely. Talk to your resources and the distributors. Is there anyone out there who could exploit your uniquenesses to the fullest as a new customer and what would they be willing to do to provide you with their expression of interest? Is the market so hot that they would provide you with a downpayment now?

Element 44, Low-Hanging Fruit *score summary:*
Weight 1 x Score 7 = Total 7

CONCLUSION OF THE COIN-OPERATED LAUNDRY

It's time to complete the Innovator's Scorecard. For the 44 Scorecard elements, we multiply each element's score by its weight factor. Taking the sum of the 44 weighted scores and dividing it by 860 (the maximum score possible) gives us our score as a percentage of the maximum. (See Appendix V for the scoring details.) This percentage indicates whether we should move forward with our business or whether we need to dig deeper.

The first cut on this business is a very respectable 57.09%. Now we go over the low scores to determine how and where to make adjustments necessary to bring your little business into reality. Yes, you flunked, but not so badly that you need to abandon the idea, yet.

Here are your flunking scores:

a   Is there a compelling unserved need (5)?

b   Is there an explainable uniqueness (6)?

c   Is there a sustainable differentiation (3)?

d   Is there bad competition (0)?

e   Is there compelling pricing possible (0)?

f   What is the quality of evidence of demand (5)?

g   Are you ahead of the market (5)?

h   Is there exposure to ambush (–5)?

i   Is there a "hot" market for your product (2)?

j   What is the commitment of the entrepreneur (6)?

k   What is the staying power of the entrepreneur (6)?

l   What is the competence of the management (4)?

m   What is the success ethic of management (6)?

n   Do you look good in the lobby (6)?

o   Does your revenue model swamp costs (6)?

p   Can you preempt and dominate the market (5)?

q   Can you establish proprietary ownership (5)?

r   What is the quality of your backup plan (3)?

s   What is the quality of your unfair advantage (2)?

t   Is this a high potential value opportunity (2)?

u   Are you pretending not to know something important (6)?

In my experience this is not necessarily a bad score. Anything under a 50% probably should be abandoned now. However, you will need to do more homework before you can roll it out for support by your critical financial and legal resources. Drive the score up into the passing zone (certainly above a 70% and if possible above an 80%) before you inspire support from a family/friend seed investor, a law firm or any others who would deliver anything of value to your enterprise. If you cannot exceed a decent passing score, but you are truly smitten with your idea, try to find someone else to carry the financial risk and burden, now, up front.

Dr. Market's Observation:

 Here's an added point about the Innovator's Scorecard, one that's important to understand but impossible to see without scoring a variety of different opportunities simultaneously: This tool changes complexion dramatically with each new idea. Some elements that are overlapping or irrelevant in one idea are significantly different or strategically imperative in another idea. Once you have used the tool frequently you will understand its uncanny strengths and wisdom in directing you toward a successful launch.

Part III

THE SCORECARD
AND BEYOND

Information in a Perfect World

If all great ideas are worth their weight in gold, how can we add the weight necessary to allow them to mature into great business opportunities? This process begins moments after the epiphany, that time when the entrepreneur encounters a thought that could be valuable. It is at that moment that key business information would be useful to the entrepreneur. Without that information, the story simply could not be adequately told so that the entrepreneur could attract capital and other resources necessary to move forward. Right?

So far we have examined many of the things that can be guessed intuitively. We understand the Innovator's Scorecard. In each element we paused to inquire about why we had selected it for consideration. Now comes the most enjoyable question, the one that I love to use in my classes. What's missing? What more could we ask, what have we not asked, and why didn't we ask for it? For the sake of setting the table for what is to come, let's aim high. What is the perfect world of information that we would love to ask of the entrepreneur so that we could make an objective decision on whether or not to invest?

As we proceed through the inventory of information that some view as sine qua non to investing, a critical problem will emerge. Let's first examine what would be wonderful to know—note that for financial services professionals, these questions will have a ring of familiarity. The "problem" should bloom before our eyes.

1. Customers and demand

The first and perhaps most important question is who are the customers and what is the intensity of demand for your product? How many customers are there? How much of your product will they purchase? How often will they purchase? What is the typical quantity of purchase? What price would satisfy their demand and offer you a decent margin? Where are the customers? How many are certain to purchase your product today? Where will they expect delivery?

2. Expected user benefits and the features necessary to deliver

What are the benefits expected by the user? What product features will deliver those benefits? What are the priorities? What features could be foregone or traded off? What are the costs of each bell and whistle? What features are easiest for you to provide while at the same time most difficult for the competition?

3. Value added

What value does your product add to the customer's enjoyment, advantage, or process? After having accumulated the costs of all resources that result in the delivery of the product to the customer, and after having factored in the price and other values that come your way, what is the difference? It is permissible here to consider all costs and all values received. Can you accurately forecast the value that will be added? Can you describe that added value in terms more fulsome than simply the calculation of your anticipated earnings?

4. Market structure

Is the market diversified or consolidated? Is it local, regional, national, or international? Are wholesalers critical to the sales and distribution process? How much control is exerted by the wholesalers and distributors, that is, can they be circumvented? Is your product destined for the hands of a retail consumer or will it be an outsourced part destined for a larger assembly or ensemble of products? What are the other complementary aspects of the market in which your product will find itself?

5. Scale

Is the size of the market sufficient to sustain the business? What is the most appropriate scale your business needs to reach in order to achieve long-term success? How does that scale compare with the size of the market? What assumptions are you making about your competition and the share of the market that must be accommodated if you are to succeed?

6. Growth potential

Is there sufficient residual demand to sustain adequate growth after the initial market penetration? Will success have anywhere to grow or compound itself or will the business find itself quickly on the far side of the maturity curve?

7. Share potential

What proportion of the market will be "owned" by the venture? Is it possible for that share to reach 100%? What are the substitutes being purchased today?

8. Market and production cost structure

How will this enterprise compare with the competition in respect to all costs, fixed and marginal? How do debt and interest expenses figure into the picture?

9. Profits after taxes

What are the expected earnings across the next five years? Are there any soft spots in the numbers?

10. ROI (return on investment)

What ROI can we anticipate across the next five years?

11. Capital

What are the anticipated precise capital requirements across the next five years, particularly prelaunch, launch, and first-year working capital?

12. IRR (internal rate of return)

What is the expected internal rate of return across the next five years on each investment of capital?

13. Cash flow

What are the anticipated cash flows across the next five years?

14. R&D (research and development)

What R&D expenditures are likely over the next five years?

15. Margins

What are the margin characteristics across the next five years?

16. Time to break even

How long until operating and overall financial break even?

17. Valuation comparables

What are the comparable sales prices for other companies in this market?

18. Capital markets

Are the capital markets adequate to sustain the investment?

19. Pricing

Is the pricing sufficiently low to ensure significant market penetration yet high enough to to recompense the shareholders?

20. Distribution

Is the distribution adequate to sustain the enterprise? Will the distribution chain cooperate with you as you attempt to launch?

21. Proprietary protection

Can the enterprise be protected by any proprietary means?

22. Lead times

Are the lead times sufficiently short to allow for timely successes?

23. Legal

Is the legal infrastructure adequately composed to protect the company? Are the lawyers licensed in the state and active in the relevant areas of the law? Are there conflicts of interest? Must you surrender too much information to learn of the conflict and will they keep your secret?

24. Contractual

Is it possible to adequately contract for the goods, services, and talent required to deliver the products on time and make this enterprise viable?

25. Contacts

Are the owners and their team sufficiently well networked to allow for fast exploitation of opportunities and deflection of threats into assets or opportunities?

26. Key personnel

Can all critical executive positions be filled? By whom? When?

27. Experience

Are the managers sufficiently experienced to accomplish their objectives and make the venture a success?

28. Integrity

Does the management have a reputation for integrity and honesty? Can you learn these matters without compromising your sources?

29. Desirability

Are the managers suitable for an entrepreneurial existence? Have they spent too much time in the ivory towers of corporate America?

30. Tolerance

What are the managers' tolerances for the ambiguities and stress associated with a new venture startup?

31. Timing

Are there any adverse timing issues regarding a launch now? This would include management, product, competition, consumers, etc.

32. Technology

Are there technology issues in evidence such as imminence of competitive threat, frailty of proprietary technology, or inability to compete?

33. Flexibility

Are the managers, board, and vendors sufficiently flexible to maneuver quickly and nimbly between surprise threats and opportunities?

34. Production

Can this product be crafted and delivered in a timely manner at a cost below the optimum sales price?

Obviously this is not an exhaustive list. However, for our purposes it will suffice.

Now for the problem that has by now become obvious. These 34 items represent the perfect world! By the time these matters are raised and resolved you will have burned off many hundreds of thousands of dollars in support costs for in-depth research and analysis. It is naïve to believe that this information will be available in any manner that could be useful within any practicable time soon.

You may be wondering why we didn't add these elements to the Innovator's Scorecard. These questions represent the *objective* Scorecard, not the **subjective** one.

GAME CAUTION

It is a remarkable time in America's corporate financial management and every book written on business matters today needs to address the appalling circumstances found in Enron, WorldCom, Tyco, and the entire financial accounting regime of our industrial society. It is possible that the tentacles of this ethics monster will reach far deeper into corporate America than is now evident. It is also possible that if we escape a broad collapse in confidence with depression to follow, we will be dumb lucky. In light of the ethics whirlwind that has erupted, there are some features of the Innovator's Scorecard that require special attention.

There is need for a Game Caution, as the soccer referees would admonish. A number of the items in the Scorecard need to be retracted over time, much like a set of flaps on an airplane as it takes off. We now understand the various elements of the Scorecard and how they fit into the puzzle of launching a thought into the market. Now try to use the items for a fully mature enterprise.

The Scorecard holds up well as your company matures. Out of 44 items, at least three are worthy of attention to retract or reduce over time.

1. *Preempting and dominating* a market could someday invite scrutiny from the Department of Justice. This moment is defined by the scale of the market under DOJ guidelines—it's OK to preempt and dominate the market in newly patented model train switches (it's new technology and the market scale is less than tiny) whereas it might be quite the contrary in the market for Internet servers.

2. Another element worthy of review is *passion*, at least that aspect of passion that is blind to reality, practicality, and ethics. I imagine that most of the bad-actors in the most notorious cases would recoil at their conduct with added maturity and seasoning. Their behavior truly was appalling. Blind passion loses its grasp of reason, dignity, grace, and sensitivity to the needs and aspirations of others. It also injects a measure of hubris—they begin to think that they are above the law. For example, several tough business development officers found themselves telling acquisition targets that they must surrender their companies or suffer demolition by the huge, new, technology-driven titans. In other cases, Ivy League educated and McKinsey trained senior executives found themselves in such a corner that they responded to legitimate investment banker questions with obscene expletives. The point is that these people knew better and yet their passion

blinded them into doing something appalling. Note that these events are not made up—they actually happened.[1]

3. *Commitment* is also an element that serves the enterprise well in the early stages of a company's development. Ironically, as a company matures, a commitment held in the form of an option held by the executive (this is how corporations often win the commitment of their executives) is a corrosive additive during times of market turmoil—keeping the option prices above water inspires legal corner cutting. Lawyers have trained us how to parse words so that all conduct short of physical abuse can be explained away when the management absolutely, positively must deliver a positive earnings picture. This propellant is double barreled—they need to keep their jobs and the financial reward resting in their options can only bloom if the numbers are higher.

This Game Caution is issued now, not because it is timely, but because you need to remember that someday you may need to adjust your conduct. When? Here are a few candidates but remember again that these matters are reserved for treatment at another time:

1. Break even

2. Tax bills due and owing

3. Season leading up to and during the issuance of your IPO

4. Post-launch solicitation of funding

Finally it could be helpful to note that solid results can be accumulated by firms that continue to preempt and dominate, hand out

---

1. The May 12, 2003, edition of *USA TODAY* carried an article called "Experts Say Founders Traits Can Lead to Trouble" by Matt Krantz where greed, irrational attachment, and corporate culture cultism were cited as primary types of conduct of which founders who remain as CEOs are often guilty. This is what failure to heed the Game Caution looks and feels like after a number of years of successful entrepreneurship.

options, and engage in blind passion. The point here is that there are right ways and wrong ways to go about it once you have reached a critical mass. *Listen* to your lawyer and your accountant and don't browbeat them into submission or you too can end up "doing time" in a federal or state penal institution.

Dr. Market's Observation:

 Actually, these people at Enron, Tyco, WorldCom, and others are qualifying for double-digit IQs (remember, you have a *three*-digit IQ). They ought to be ousted because they were so d-u-m-b (I suspect that even they would agree just now). Among other stupid behavior, they were pretending to believe that there would be no due diligence by qualified investment bankers. Their conduct was guaranteed to catch up with them, even if they coerced the auditor/accounting firm to roll along with them for a few days. The only true salvation for our corporate financial reporting system is the assurance that sooner or later, fraud is certain to catch up with perpetrators, almost certainly during the next capitalization round when large sums of cash need to be raised. That's when the good investment banks would see enough to smell a rat. You may ask why an investment bank cares, just so long as it moves the money and pockets the commission. If there is a revelation that there are material flaws in the financial picture, they who are out on the limb for underwriting and guaranteeing financial authenticity (the investment banks are required to stand behind their deals—perhaps in justification for their use of the term "bank") lose *their* shirts, just like you do if your business refuses to fly.

CONCLUSION

There are thousands of things that must be considered and mastered in launching new ventures.[1] The majority of them are not relevant until the resources and distribution have matured somewhat and the level of thinking and operations is far more sophisticated. The elements in the Scorecard are the matters that you can evaluate intuitively, up front. They are also excellent alignment tools for the enterprise at large, allowing you to position your idea for the optimum chance of success. Nearly all of the items survive the launch process quite well. However, while some of the more aggressive elements are particularly useful in

---

1. Jeffry Timmons believes that the actual number is more like 50,000. See *New Venture Creation*, 5th edition, p. 46, Irwin-McGraw Hill, 1999.

315

lifting your venture off of the ground, they should be eliminated or greatly tempered when the company matures.

Sooner or later you will need to begin sharing your idea with others. You cannot keep your idea under a teacup. This does not give you license to explain your idea to everyone you see willy nilly. Be careful. Use this tool, spot your weaknesses now, drive the score up, and inch your way into the marketplace. Your first job is to attract the resources necessary to elevate the score. Almost immediately you will need to find a lawyer who can help you protect your intellectual property, your idea. You will also need to address the roster on your management team—most investors place e-x-t-r-a-o-r-d-i-n-a-r-y weight on it. Now that you have aligned your idea for success, you need to follow through, a ripe subject for treatment in our next "conversation."

Dr. Market's Final Observation:

How about a fun twist? If you can raise, evaluate, and put to rest a large number of ideas quickly, the Innovator's Scorecard becomes a tool that can be used often to sift through many different opportunities in a very short period of time. It becomes an effective weapon in conquering strategic opponents by allowing you to constantly monitor the marketplace for ideas that could be quite profitable. Keep the Scorecard handy and use it often. It'll make your family, friends, employees, brokers, bankers, money managers, gardeners, premium auto dealers, country club managers, yacht salesmen, spas, private school treasurers, clothiers, and alma maters all genuinely and sincerely happy about their ever having met you.

Carpe diem!

Appendix I

ORION SATELLITE CORPORATION

In 1982, it was apparent that the cost of moving television and voice signals (data was still largely something yet to unfold) across an ocean via satellite was roughly ten times higher than in the domestic United States. It was, after all, the same technology at work. The only difference was that the transoceanic international satellite technology being used belonged to Intelsat, the cartel situated in Washington and accessed through Comsat. On March 11, 1983, Orion filed its application at the FCC on a day when all of the Intelsat board of directors members were in the air heading for a lavish meeting in Australia. Before they could organize a summary rejection by the FCC, the application was "accepted for filing," and the legal battle was joined. The original team consisted of the author plus Christopher Vizas and Thomas Keller—three law-educated friends who met at The White House Office of Telecommunications Policy, and a typewriter (this remark was one made by the director general of Intelsat when he was trying to defeat us). Financial backing came from Denver and the charge was led by John Saeman, Gus Hauser, and Steve Halstedt. On September 15, 1985, the FCC made its preliminary decision that ultimately led to nearly full authority for us and our "me-too" competitor, PanAmSat, to operate our satellites. The company proceeded to design, build, launch, and operate its satellites and its services are available today from the Mississippi to Moscow. John Puente, the seasoned veteran from Macom, arrived and managed the financing and launch and later retired. We went public in 1995 and soon thereafter we were acquired by Loral. Again, a special thanks to Ward L. Quaal, a truly great American, and of course our president, Ronald Reagan. Thank you again, Mr. President.

Appendix II

PTAT System, Inc.

In light of the public scrutiny subjected to Orion, at a Christmas party in 1983, Jonathan Miller, a journalist of *Communications Daily* fame, taunted the author in his kitchen with the following: "McKnight, why don't you drop that satellite idea—it's just too hard! Why don't you just go undersea with a cable. There would be no opposition." In 1984 several seasoned veterans of the telecommunications policy game in Washington listened to Brian Hughes (also present in Jonathan's kitchen) explain that an undersea fiber optic cable could circumvent the policy and legal thicket encountered by Orion and succeed in the private movement of telecommunications traffic to Europe. The team, led by Konnie Schaffer and Ronald Coleman, packaged, financed, designed, built, and began to install the cable stretched between New Jersey, Ireland, the UK, and France. Cable & Wireless, the British telecommunications company, volunteered to support the launch financially and delivered a cable of extraordinary quality. I was hired in 1987 to wrap the entire enterprise into a sale to an American carrier. With a seasoned veteran of the private telecommunications industry, Robert Bennis of Westinghouse, and a glib, charming, and hard-driving engineer out of MCI named Warren Liss, we embarked upon a one-year campaign that accumulated 17 written expressions of interest from Fortune 100 companies. I then approached an old colleague from my days at the FCC, Nancy Carey, who was William Esrey's special assistant and who helped align the parties for maximum success. Nancy is the one who delivered our number 2 benefit to Mr. Esrey for his use in the staff meeting (we of course withdrew the benefit from our presentation). Mr. Esrey looked brilliant in front of the staff and suddenly it was his baby. The result was a 1988 meeting with William Burgess, Sr. VP International at Sprint, which culminated in Bill's remark, "I wish to begin the bidding at 100% of your working assets." Soon thereafter we closed on the sale of PTAT for $285 million cash plus all accumulated debt, 17 months before the cable was ready for service.

Appendix III

CREATIVE DESTRUCTION

Dr. Joseph Schumpeter. Capitalism, Socialism, and Democracy, pp. 82–85, Harper 1975, quoting the original which was published in 1942:

The opening up of new markets, foreign or domestic, and the organizational development from the craft shop and factory to such concerns as US Steel illustrate the same process of industrial mutation if I may use that biological term that incessantly revolutionizes the economic structure *from within*, incessantly destroying the old one, incessantly creating a new one. This process of Creative Destruction is the essential fact about capitalism. It is what capitalism consists in and what every capitalist concern has got to live in...

Every piece of business strategy acquires its true significance only against the background of that process and within the situation created by it. It must be seen in its role in the perennial gale of creative destruction. . .

Appendix IV

INNOVATOR'S
SCORECARD

All scores are 10s and the aggregate points are 860. Innovator's Scorecard for spotting a winning launch opportunity (pre-research and pre-business plan analysis).

Grade   100%

	Criteria	Raw Score (–10 to +10)	Weight	Total
1	Compelling Unserved Need	10	3	30
2	Explainable Uniqueness	10	3	30
3	Sustainable Differentiation	10	1	10
4	Demonstrable Now	10	1	10

	Criteria	Raw Score (−10 to +10)	Weight	Total
5	Good Competition	10	2	20
6	Bad Competition	10	3	30
7	Compelling Pricing Possible	10	1	10
8	Closable Customers	10	2	20
9	Quality Of Evidence Of Demand	10	2	20
10	Ahead Of Market	10	2	20
11	Ambush Exposure	10	3	30
12	"Hot Market"	10	1	10
13	Attitude: Confidence And Fearlessness	10	2	20
14	Commitment	10	3	30
15	Staying Power	10	2	20
16	Passion	10	1	10
17	Management Competence	10	3	30
18	Honest and Integrity	10	3	30
19	Success Ethic	10	2	20
20	Looking Good in the Lobby	10	1	10
21	Cash Flowing Now	10	2	20
22	Revenue Model Swamps Costs	10	1	10
23	Delivery Advantages	10	1	10
24	Resources Available	10	3	30
25	Preemption and Domination	10	1	10
26	Strategy to Penetrate Market	10	2	20
27	Strategy for Breaching the Chasm	10	1	10
28	Proprietary Ownership	10	3	30
29	Partnering Candidates	10	1	10
30	Appropriateness of Location	10	2	20

	Criteria	Raw Score (–10 to +10)	Weight	Total
31	Quality of Backup Plan	10	1	10
32	Unfair Advantages	10	3	30
33	Manageable Capital Requirements	10	3	30
34	Low Cash Required Prelaunch	10	2	20
35	Visible Capital	10	1	10
36	High Potential Value	10	3	30
37	Foreseeable Harvest?	10	1	10
38	Taboo	10	2	20
39	Lack of Showstoppers	10	3	30
40	Pretending Not to Know	10	1	10
41	High-Profile Persons Available	10	2	20
42	Punchy, Compelling Story	10	3	30
43	Government Relevance	10	2	20
44	Low-Hanging Fruit	10	1	10
	TOTAL	440		860

© 2000, 2001, 2002, 2003, Thomas McKnight.
(Last update 1-22-03.)

Appendix V

COIN-OPERATED LAUNDRY EXAMPLE

Aperture for spotting a winning launch opportunity (Cleaners and Laundry Example).

Grade   57.09%

	Criteria	Raw Score (–10 to +10)	Weight	Total
1	Compelling Unserved Need	5	3	15
2	Explainable Uniqueness	6	3	18
3	Sustainable Differentiation	3	1	3
4	Demonstrable Now	8	1	8
5	Good Competition	10	2	20

	Criteria	Raw Score (−10 to +10)	Weight	Total
6	Bad Competition	0	3	0
7	Compelling Pricing Possible	0	1	0
8	Closable Customers	10	2	20
9	Quality Of Evidence Of Demand	5	2	10
10	Ahead Of Market	5	2	10
11	Ambush Exposure	−5	3	−15
12	"Hot Market"	2	1	2
13	Attitude: Confidence And Fearlessness	7	2	14
14	Commitment	6	3	18
15	Staying Power	6	2	12
16	Passion	7	1	7
17	Management Competence	4	3	12
18	Honest and Integrity	8	3	24
19	Success Ethic	6	2	12
20	Looking Good in the Lobby	6	1	6
21	Cash Flowing Now	7	2	14
22	Revenue Model Swamps Costs	6	1	6
23	Delivery Advantages	7	1	7
24	Resources Available	7	3	21
25	Preemption and Domination	5	1	5
26	Strategy to Penetrate Market	7	2	14
27	Strategy for Breaching the Chasm	7	1	7
28	Proprietary Ownership	5	3	15
29	Partnering Candidates	8	1	8
30	Appropriateness of Location	8	2	16
31	Quality of Backup Plan	3	1	3

	Criteria	Raw Score (−10 to +10)	Weight	Total
32	Unfair Advantages	2	3	6
33	Manageable Capital Requirements	8	3	24
34	Low Cash Required Prelaunch	8	2	16
35	Visible Capital	9	1	9
36	High Potential Value	2	3	6
37	Foreseeable Harvest?	9	1	9
38	Taboo	10	2	20
39	Lack of Showstoppers	7	3	21
40	Pretending Not to Know	6	1	6
41	High-Profile Persons Available	7	2	14
42	Punchy, Compelling Story	7	3	21
43	Government Relevance	10	2	20
44	Low-Hanging Fruit	7	1	7
	TOTAL	261		491

ABOUT THE AUTHOR

Thomas K. McKnight grew up in Cincinnati and still roots for the Reds, the Redhawks (B.S. in Business from Miami University), and the Buckeyes (J.D., The Ohio State University). In the Marines, he was a bench technician whose job it was to breathe life back into radar equipment that had been abused, blown up, or dropped from aircraft. He was a lawyer at the FCC in a bureau that attempted to strangle a new industry (cable) to protect an old one (television broadcast). At the White House, he helped provide legal cover for a group of senior military officers who were nervous about national security and electronic communications. He became a broadcast attorney for an awe-inspiring team of entrepreneurs at Combined Communications Corporation (Karl Eller, Larry Wilson, Al Flanagan, and Jeff Davidson). Gannett acquired Combined and McKnight helped USA Today as it was launched by the indomitable Al Neuharth. McKnight launched his own entrepreneurial career with Orion Satellite Corporation. Other highlights include PTAT and Smith Barney (he's still a licensed stock broker). Since 1996, he has been teaching entrepreneurship courses at Columbia University, Georgetown, Maryland, George Washington, American, Denver, and the University of North Dakota. In 1997, he was Entrepreneur in Residence, The Wharton School, University of Pennsylvania. He has worked or done business in 23 countries. He is currently involved in the growth and development of a new mortgage-lending institution and the dramatic expansion of a buy-renovate-rent residential real property enterprise in the Washington, D.C. metro area.

He can be reached at innovators-scorecard@thomasmcknight.net.

INDEX

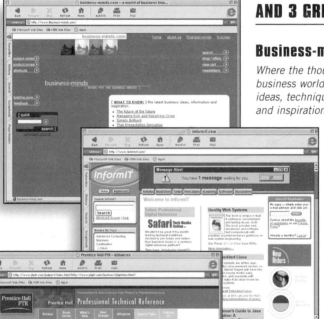